DATE DUE

~~JAN 0 3 1994~~		
~~JUL 0 5 1995~~		
ILL CGA		
~~40757374~~		
4/13/08		

DEMCO 38-297

Job
The Victim
of His People

Job
The Victim
of His People

RENÉ GIRARD

Translated by
YVONNE FRECCERO

STANFORD UNIVERSITY PRESS
STANFORD, CALIFORNIA
1987

Stanford University Press
Stanford, California
© 1985 Editions Grasset & Fasquelle
English translation © 1987 The Athlone Press
Originally published in French 1985 by
Editions Grasset & Fasquelle as
La route antique des hommes pervers
Originating publisher of English edition:
The Athlone Press, London
First published in the U.S.A. by
Stanford University Press, 1987
Printed in Great Britain
ISBN 0-8047-1404-5
LC 86–63896

Contents

I
THE CASE OF JOB

1

Job the Victim of his People

What do we know about the Book of Job? Not very much. The hero complains endlessly. He has just lost his children and all his livestock. He scratches his ulcers. The misfortunes of which he complains are all duly enumerated in the prologue. They are misfortunes brought on him by Satan with God's permission.

We think we know, but are we sure? Not once in the Dialogues does Job mention either Satan or anything about his misdeeds. Could it be that they are too much on his mind for him to mention them?

Possibly, yet Job mentions everything else, and does much more than mention. He dwells heavily on the cause of his misfortune, which is none of those mentioned in the prologue. The cause is not divine, satanic nor physical, but merely human.

Strangely enough, over the centuries commentators have not paid the slightest attention to that cause. I am not familiar with all the commentaries, naturally, but those I do know systematically ignore it. They seem not to notice it. Ancients and moderns alike, atheists, Protestants, Catholics or Jews – none of them questions the object of Job's complaints. The matter seems to have been settled for them in the prologue. Everyone clings religiously to the ulcers, the lost cattle, etc.

And yet exegetes have been warning their readers for some time about this prologue. This short narrative is not on the same level as the Dialogues and should not be taken seriously. Unfortunately they do not follow their own advice. They pay

In the preparation of this translation, the translator and Publishers are grateful for the advice provided by Professor Paisley Livingston.

no attention to the parts of the Dialogues that clearly contradict the prologue.

The new element I am suggesting is not buried in an obscure corner of the Book of Job. It is very explicit and is apparent in numerous and copious passages that are not in the least equivocal.

Job clearly articulates the cause of his suffering – the fact that he is ostracized and persecuted by the people around him. He has done no harm, yet everyone turns away from him and is dead set against him. He is the scapegoat of his community:

> My brothers stand aloof from me,
>   and my relations take care to avoid me.
> My kindred and my friends have all gone away,
>   and the guests in my house have forgotten me.
> The serving maids look on me as a foreigner,
>   a stranger, never seen before.
> My servant does not answer when I call him,
>   I am reduced to entreating him.
> To my wife my breath is unbearable,
>   for my own brothers I am a thing corrupt.
> Even the children look down on me,
>   ever ready with a gibe when I appear.
> All my dearest friends recoil from me in horror:
>   those I loved best have turned against me. (19: 13–19,
>   *The Jerusalem Bible*)

Even the fact that Job's wife complains of his foul breath reminds us of the tragic goat, a significant detail found in many primitive myths.

This allusion to a real goat should not be misunderstood. When I speak of a scapegoat I am not referring to the sacrificial animal in the famous rites of Leviticus. I am using the expression in the sense in which we all use it, casually, in reference to political, professional or family matters. This is a modern usage not found, of course, in the Book of Job. But the phenomenon is present in a more primitive form. The scapegoat is the innocent party who polarizes a universal hatred, which is precisely the complaint of Job:

> And now ill will drives me to distraction,
>   and a whole host molests me,
> rising, like some witness for the prosecution,
>   to utter slander to my very face.
> In tearing fury it pursues me,
>   with gnashing teeth.
> My enemies whet their eyes on me,
>   and open gaping jaws.
> Their insults strike like slaps in the face,
>   and all set on me together. (16: 7–10)

The text teems with such revealing passages. Since I cannot quote them all, I will choose those that are most striking in relation to my topic. One such passage introduces a subgroup that plays the role of permanent scapegoat in Job's society:

> And now I am the laughing stock
>   of my juniors, the young people,
> whose fathers I did not consider fit
>   to put with the dogs that looked after my flock.
> The strength of their hands would have been useless to me,
>   enfeebled as they were,
>   worn out by want and hunger.
> They used to gnaw the roots of desert plants,
>   and brambles from abandoned ruins;
> and plucked mallow, and brushwood leaves,
>   making their meals off roots of broom.
> Outlawed from the society of men,
>   who, as against thieves, raised hue and cry against them,
> they made their dwellings on ravines' steep sides,
>   in caves or clefts in the rock.
> You could hear them wailing from the bushes,
>   as they huddled together in the thistles.

Their children are as worthless a brood as they were,
    nameless people, outcasts of society.
And these are the ones that now sing ballads about me,
    and make me the talk of the town!
To them I am loathsome, they stand aloof from me,
    do not scruple to spit in my face.
Because he has unbent my bow and chastened me
    they cast the bridle from their mouth.
That brood of theirs rises to right of me,
    stones are their weapons . . . (30: 1–12)

Historians do not know whether this group of scapegoats is a racial or religious minority, or some kind of sub-proletariat subjected to the same sort of regime as the lowest castes in India. It is not important. These people are not interesting in themselves; they are there only for Job to compare himself with them and define himself as the scapegoat of these scapegoats, persecuted by those who could least indulge in persecution, the victim of absolutely everyone, the scapegoat of scapegoats, the victim of victims.

The more obstinately Job remains silent on the subject of his lost cattle and his other good reasons for complaint, the more he insists on portraying himself as the innocent victim of those around him.

It is true that Job complains of physical ills, but this particular complaint is easily linked to the basic cause of his lament. He is the victim of countless brutalities; the psychological pressure on him is unbearable.

Some would say that Job's life is not really threatened, and that there is no question of killing him. He is protected by his friends. This is absolutely false. Job thinks they are after his life, and he may think that it is particularly his life they are after. He expects to die soon, and not from the illness that his doctors are struggling to diagnose. He thinks he is going to die a violent death: he imagines the shedding of his own blood:

Cover not my blood, O earth,
    afford my cry no place to rest. (16: 18)

I am content with the interpretation of these two lines given in *The Jerusalem Bible* footnotes: 'Blood, if not covered with earth, cries to heaven for vengeance [. . .] Job, mortally wounded, wishes to leave behind a lasting appeal for vindication: on earth, his blood; with God, the sound of his prayer . . .'

The translation of the two lines and the footnote conform exactly to what is found in the other great translations. The language of the footnote, granted, is somewhat ambiguous. By whom is Job wounded to death? It could just be by God rather than by men, but it certainly is not against God that the blood of the victim cries for vengeance; he is crying to God for vengeance, like the blood of Abel, that first great victim exhumed by the Bible. Yahweh says to Cain: 'Listen to the sound of your brother's blood, crying out to me from the ground' (Genesis 4: 10).

But against whom is the blood that is shed crying for vengeance? Who would seek to stifle the cries of Job, erase his words to prevent them from reaching God? Strangely enough, these elementary questions have never been asked.

Job constantly reverts to the community's role in what has happened to him, but – and this is what is mysterious – he does not succeed in making his commentators, outside the text, understand him any better than those who question him within the text . . . No one takes any notice of what he says.

The revelation of the scapegoat is as nonexistent for posterity as it is for his friends. Yet we are really trying to be attentive to what Job is saying; we pity him for not being understood. But we are so afraid of holding God accountable for all man's misfortunes, especially if we do not believe in him, that ultimately the result is the same. We are just a little more hypocritical than Job's friends. For all those who have always appeared to listen to Job but have not understood him, his words are so much air. The only difference is that we dare not express our indifference, as his friends did:

Is there no end to these words of yours,
to your long-winded blustering? (8: 2)

The victim's role that Job claims is bound to be significant
within a collection of texts like the Bible where victims,
always and everywhere, are prominent. On further reflection,
it becomes apparent that the reason for the astonishing
similarity between Job's discourse and what we call the
penitential Psalms can be found in the perspective common
to victims surrounded by numerous enemies.

Raymund Schwager's book[1] provides an excellent reference on the topic of the tragic Psalms. These texts describe, in an extremely condensed form, the situation found
in Job's complaints: an innocent victim, usually of a lynching,
is speaking. Raymund Schwager is not mistaken: a scapegoat
in the modern sense is describing the cruelties he is made to
endure. There is one enormous difference. In the Psalms,
only the victim speaks; in the Dialogues of Job, other voices
make themselves heard.

Because the texts I have just mentioned best describe Job
as scapegoat, they are also those which most resemble the
Psalms. In fact they are so similar that they are interchangeable. Each focuses on the surrogate victim, that
powerful element shared in common by so many biblical
texts yet mysteriously ignored by everyone. There is no
doubt that the intellectual expulsion of this scapegoat victim
is the continuation of the physical violence of antiquity.

An excellent way to dispel the erroneous influence of the
prologue, and come to terms with what Job is really about, is
to reread the Psalms:

To every one of my oppressors
  I am contemptible,
loathsome to my neighbours,
  to my friends a thing of fear.

Those who see me in the street
  hurry past me;
I am forgotten, as good as dead in their hearts,
  something discarded.

I hear their endless slanders,
  threats from every quarter,
as they combine against me,
  plotting to take my life. (Psalms 31: 11–13)

2

Job the Idol of his People

Why has Job become the object of hatred for his community? No direct answer is given. Perhaps it is better this way. If the author were to identify a precise element or mention a certain incident as the possible origin, no matter what, we would immediately think we knew the answer and stop questioning. In reality we would know less than ever.

But we must not assume that the Dialogues are completely silent. They are full of indications, if we know where to look for them. In our search for an explanation of the choice of Job as a scapegoat, we should not ask just anyone. His 'friends', for example, have nothing interesting to say on the subject. They want to make Job responsible for the cruelties he is made to endure. They suggest that his avarice was his undoing; perhaps he was harsh to his people and used his position to exploit the poor and the weak.

Job appears to be virtuous but maybe, like Oedipus, he has committed a hidden crime. Or perhaps his son or some other member of his family has done so. A man condemned by the voice of the people could hardly be innocent. But Job defends himself so vigorously that no accusation holds. The indictments gradually fade away.

Some commentators reproach Job for his vigorous self-defence. He lacks humility and his friends are right to be scandalized. Such a reproach completely misunderstands the nature of the debate. Job's indignation must be put in its proper context, as he himself defines it, to be understood.

He does not say that he has never sinned, he says he has done nothing that deserves his extreme disgrace; just yesterday he could do no wrong and was treated like a saint, now everyone is against him. It is not he who has changed but the people around him. The Job that everyone detests cannot be much different from the man everyone revered.

The Job of the Dialogues is not just somebody who made a lot of money and then lost it all. He is not just a person who goes from splendour to misery and decides to talk over with his friends the attributes of God and the metaphysics of evil. The Job of the Dialogues is not the Job of the prologue. He is a great leader who at first commands the respect of the people and is then abruptly scorned by them:

Who will bring back to me the months that have gone,
  [. . .]
when my feet were plunged in cream,
    and streams of oil poured from the rocks?
When I went out to the gate of the city,
    when I took my seat in the square,
as soon as I appeared, the young men stepped aside,
    while the older men rose to their feet.
Men of note interrupted their speeches,
    and put their fingers on their lips;
the voices of rulers were silenced,
    and their tongues stayed still in their mouths.
They waited anxiously to hear me,
    and listened in silence to what I had to say.
When I paused, there was no rejoinder,
    and my words dropped on them, one by one.
They waited for me, as men wait for rain,
    open-mouthed, as if to catch the year's last showers.
If I smiled at them, it was too good to be true,
    they watched my face for the least sign of favour.
In a lordly style, I told them which course to take,
    and like a king amid his armies,
I led them where I chose. (29: 2–25)

Before he became a scapegoat Job lived through a period of extraordinary popularity bordering on idolatry. We see clearly from this passage that the prologue has no relevance at all. If Job had really lost his cattle and his children, his reminiscence about the past would have provided the opportunity to mention that loss. But there is no reference to it . . .

The contrast between past and present is not from riches to poverty, or from health to sickness, but from favour to disfavour with the very same people. The Dialogues are not dealing with a purely personal drama or a simple change of circumstance, but with the behaviour of all the people towards a statesman whose career has been destroyed.

The accusations against Job, no matter how questionable, are very revealing. Primarily, the fallen potentate is reproached for abusing his power: an accusation that could not be made against any ordinary landowner, however rich. Job reminds us of the *tyrant* of the Greek cities. Eliphaz asks him: Why has Shaddai turned against you?

> Would he punish you for your piety,
>   and hale you off to judgement?
> No, rather for your manifold wickednesses,
>   for your unending iniquities!
> You have exacted needless pledges from your brothers,
>   and men go naked now through your despoiling;
> you have grudged water to the thirsty man,
>   and refused bread to the hungry;
> you have narrowed the lands of the poor man down to
>   nothing
>   to set your crony in his place,
> sent widows away empty-handed
>   and crushed the arms of orphans. (22: 4–9)

We modern readers eagerly accept the vision of the prologue because it fits our own world, or at least our idea of it. Happiness consists of having as many possessions as possible without ever becoming ill, of enjoying an eternal frenzy of consumer pleasure. In the Dialogues, on the other hand, the only thing that counts is Job's relationship with the community.

Job portrays his triumphal period as the autumn of his life –
in other words, the season that immediately precedes the icy
winter of persecution. The disgrace was probably recent and
very sudden. The extreme infatuation with Job suddenly
turned into extreme disgust. Job seems to have had no
warning of the sudden change that was about to take place:

> My praises echoed in every ear,
>   and never an eye but smiled on me;
> because I freed the poor man when he called,
>   and the orphan who had no one to help him . . .
>
> So I thought to myself, 'I shall die in honour,
>   my days like a palm tree's for number.
> My roots thrust out to the water,
>   my leaves freshened by the falling dew at night.
> My reputation will never fade,
>   and the bow in my hands will gain new strength.' (29)

The mystery of Job is presented in a context that does not
explain it but at least allows us to situate it. The scapegoat is a
shattered idol. The rise and fall of Job are bound up in one
another. The two extremes seem to be connected. They cannot
be understood separately, and yet one is not the cause of the
other. We sense an ill-defined but very real social phenomenon
in the probable unfolding of events.

The one thing in common between the two periods is the
community's unanimity: first in worship, then later in
loathing. Job is the victim of a huge and sudden reversal of
public opinion that is obviously unstable, capricious and void
of all moderation. He seems hardly more responsible for the
change in this crowd than Jesus is for a similar change between
Palm Sunday and Good Friday.

For this dual unanimity to exist, the mimetic contagion of
the crowd must be at work. Members of the community
influence each other reciprocally; they imitate each other in
fanatical worship and then in even more fanatical hostility.

3

The Ancient Trail Trodden by the Wicked

In the last of the three Dialogues Eliphaz of Teman, one of the three friends, clearly alludes to the existence of predecessors of Job who were both powerful upstarts and scapegoats:

> And will you still follow the ancient trail
>   trodden by the wicked?
> Those men who were borne off before their time,
>   with rivers swamping their foundations,
> because they said to God, 'Go away!
>   What can Shaddai do to us?'
> Yet he himself had filled their houses with good things
>   while these wicked men shut him out of their counsels.
> At the sight of their ruin, good men rejoice,
>   and the innocent deride them:
> 'See how their greatness is brought to nothing!
>   See how their wealth has perished in the flames!' (22: 15–20)

The 'ancient trail trodden by the wicked' begins with grandeur, riches and power but ends in overwhelming disaster. We have just observed these same two phases, the identical scenario, in the experience of Job.

Some day soon Job may well figure on the list of these anonymous men, who are hinted at only because their name has been 'erased'. He is one of those whose career is likely to end badly because it began too well.

Just as I have done, Eliphaz contrasts and, inevitably, compares the two phases. He recognizes that they form a whole and cannot be interpreted separately. Something in the rise of these men contributes to their fall. Our every intuition is voiced in the words of Eliphaz. Job has already travelled quite a distance along the 'ancient trail [of] the wicked'. He has reached the beginning of the final stage.

The events recalled by Eliphaz seem distant and therefore unusual, but not so unusual as to prevent the observer from recognizing in them a recurring phenomenon. The path has already been traced: many men have already taken it and now it is Job's turn. All these tragic destinies share the characteristic profile of the shattered idol. Their destiny, like Job's, is inevitably determined by the transformation of a crowd of worshippers into a crowd of persecutors.

Eliphaz could not allude to events in the *past*, if the disasters of wicked men were imaginary. He must be evoking an experience that everyone knows because it belongs to the entire community. The violent downfall of the wicked is alive in everyone's memory. These reversals leave too deep an impression to be forgotten, and their stereotypical character makes them easy to remember.

In the eyes of Eliphaz and of the community, the 'wickedness' of these victims is clearly demonstrated, just like Job's guilt. Once they have been denied by the crowd, former idols can never justify themselves; the poor unfortunates are condemned once and for all. The unanimity that is now formed against Job must have also been formed against them in earlier times.

The same process is beginning again and Eliphaz's warning is justified. Job would do well to pay attention to the words of this wise man. But how can he do so without abjuring himself and admitting his guilt?

Perhaps Eliphaz reproaches himself for having been too friendly with the criminal he considers Job to be. He speaks quite openly of the trial of popular 'justice' which, far from being a reprehensible act of disorder, seems legitimate to him, infallible and, quite literally, divine. His conscience is clear and he finds everything to be in order. The order is perfect, and the three 'friends' are happy that it has been forcefully reaffirmed.

Are 'wicked' men always the victims of crowd violence?
Could it be a question of anything else? Reread the last four
lines of the quotation. They allude to a violent form of social
expulsion:

> At the sight of their ruin, good men rejoice,
>   and the innocent deride them:
> 'See how their greatness is brought to nothing!
> See how their wealth has perished in the flames!'

In the context of a rural society, the 'rejoicing of good men'
and the 'derision of the innocent' are not without consequence. We must consider the formidable effect of unanimous condemnation in such an environment. To bring about
the disasters ascribed to him, a god need only leave it to these
good men, who are always ready to act in the name of his
vengeance.

In the middle of the crowd we find the victim and all his
possessions. The mob has already divided up what can be
shared; perhaps they drew lots to avoid fights. What cannot be
shared – which includes their former owner – will be con-
sumed in great fires of joy.

The disaster that awaits 'the wicked' at the final stage, at the
end of the 'ancient trail', must resemble those primitive feasts
which, in spite of their moderated and ritualistic nature, remind us of a crowd phenomenon. Such social dramas always
end with the simulated drowning or immolation of a
scapegoat. Former ethnologists sensed the existence of a more
extreme violence behind the ritual forms they observed. Many
contemporary scholars regard them as victims of their own
romantic and colonialist imagination. Yet I think that the
earlier ethnologists were right. No doubt they had their prejudices, but we also have ours; the fervent Rousseauian dogma
of today ignores the massive evidence that contradicts it, and
thus hardly inspires confidence.

There are many other passages to suggest that the central
event of the text, the terrible experience that is just beginning

for the hero, is a recurring phenomenon of collective violence that is particularly, but not exclusively, directed against the 'mighty' and the 'tyrants'. This violence is always interpreted as an act of divine vengeance, as a god's punitive intervention.

I will cite only one example. It is found in the speech of Elihu, the fourth speaker in Job. This character is not generally thought to belong to the original Dialogues. His speech is probably the work of a reader who was scandalized by the impotence of the first three guardians of public order. Elihu despises the fact that the other three are rooted in tradition and strives to succeed where they have failed.

He thinks he is more able simply because he is younger and because he despises the past. He too tries to reduce Job to silence but succeeds only in restating, in a less attractive style, what the other three have already said. He belongs to a stage in which the archaic tradition is more feeble. Nevertheless, some of what he says makes the hidden topic of the Dialogues clearer than ever.

The theme of Job 'the oppressor of his people' has already been mentioned by the three friends; Elihu sets even greater store by it. The people's violence shines through his political and religious statements.

We are told that God, in an instant:

> smashes great men's power without inquiry
> and sets up others in their places.
> He knows well enough what they are about,
> and one fine night he throws them down for men to
> trample on.
> He strikes them down for their wickedness,
> and makes them prisoners for all to see. (34: 24–6)

I am quoting from *The Jerusalem Bible*: the identity of God and the crowd are clearly suggested in the translation. God overthrows the great, but the crowd *tramples* on them. God makes prisoners of the victims, but his intervention is *for all to see*. It takes place in the presence of that same crowd, which perhaps does not remain completely passive before such an interesting spectacle. It is hardly surprising that the power of the great is smashed 'without inquiry'. The crowd is always ready to lend God a hand when he decides to take action against the wicked. Other great men are immediately found to replace those who have fallen. God himself sets them up in their places, but it is the crowd that worships them – only to discover later, of course, that they were again wrongly chosen and were no better than their predecessors.

Vox populi, vox dei. As in Greek tragedy, the rise and fall of great men constitutes a truly sacred *mystery* and its conclusion is the part most appreciated. Although it never changes, it is always anticipated with great impatience.

II
MYTHOLOGY AND TRUTH

4

The Celestial Armies

What are the three 'friends' doing in the company of the scapegoat? The prologue tells us that they are there to have pity on Job and 'console' him. Their elaborate speeches are not the least bit comforting, but the commentators attribute the harshness of the friends to their awkwardness and to the strictness of their theology. That they are truly friends is never questioned, for their intentions are always believed to be good.

No one looks closely enough at what these alleged 'friends' are saying. The first thing to strike the unsuspecting reader is the tremendous violence of their speeches. Listen to Eliphaz:

> The life of the wicked is unceasing torment,
> the years allotted to the tyrant are numbered.
> The danger signal ever echoes in his ear,
> in the midst of peace the marauder swoops on him.
> He has no hope of fleeing from the darkness,
> but he knows that he is destined for the sword,
> marked down as meat for the vulture. (15: 20–3)

There are dozens of passages like this that describe a wicked man, an oppressor of the people, who used to be powerful but is no longer. God has finally cursed him. The vengeance of the celestial armies pursues him. One of the three friends, Zophar of Naamath, describes for us the fate that awaits this mysterious 'tyrant':

On him God looses all his burning wrath,
   hurling against his flesh a hail of arrows.
No use to run away from the iron armoury,
   for the bow of bronze will shoot him through.
Out through his back an arrow sticks,
   from his gall a shining point.
An arsenal of terrors falls on him,
   and all that is dark lies in ambush for him.
A fire unlit by man devours him,
   and consumes what is left in his tent.
The heavens lay bare his iniquity,
   the earth takes its stand against him.
A flood sweeps his house away,
   and carries it off in the Day of Wrath.
Such is the fate God allots to the wicked,
   such his inheritance assigned by God. (20: 22–9)

From the perspective of the prologue, there is no justification for these threatening tirades. Why should a poor unfortunate man, overwhelmed by a series of inexplicable accidents as Job passes for being, also imagine that he is pursued by innumerable executors of a mysterious 'divine vengeance'? Why should someone who has just lost his health, his children and his fortune also provoke the formidable assemblage of hostility described by his 'friends'?

Is someone other than Job the object of these vociferations? Job is under no illusions. Point-blank, three times in a row, and in the same military order the three friends fire off their sinister and arrogant maledictions. At whom else could they be aimed? Job is not quite yet the enemy of God in question, but he could become God's enemy and certainly will, if he persists in rebelling against the unanimous voice of condemnation.

That is precisely the message of Eliphaz. He who is sometimes called 'the enemy of God', sometimes 'the accursed one' or simply 'the wretch' is merely one of 'the wicked'. For this kind of black sheep, there are five or six interchangeable labels. These speeches always bear the same threat for Job – that of collective violence, more and more of it.

In contrast to Job, whose language in the passages that describe his experience as a victim is as crudely realistic as the theme it describes, the three friends adopt a style that befits their presumed grandeur. Although there are plenty of concrete details, they are couched in the style of religious epic.

Two types of discourse must therefore be distinguished: that of the friends and that of Job. Later we shall see that this distinction is not always valid, but it certainly is for the passages I have quoted here. The distance between the complaints of the sufferer and the epic style of the friends is so great that initially it discourages any comparison. The celestial armies would seem to have nothing in common with the petty persecutions described by Job.

But if Job and his friends were not talking about the same thing, there would be no point to the Dialogues; indeed, there would be no real dialogue. The reader who does not recognize the crucial role of the scapegoat is struck by a certain general incoherence. The characters do not really talk to one another. This is particularly true of the friends, who do not seem to hear Job's complaints and arguments.

Contemporary criticism is mostly concerned with the rhetorical differences between discourses. It is less interested in what is said than in how it is said. This kind of criticism holds that to be interested in what it offhandedly calls 'the referent' is to stray from 'the literary' – yet in the final analysis, this attitude is responsible for the misunderstandings that surround the great texts.

The exegetes of Job have never been able to discover the object that is common to the two types of discourse I have just identified. But they are still seeking it, at least in theory. What characterizes contemporary criticism, on the other hand, is the desire to give up the search.

We must not give in to this temptation. The main theme in the harangues of the friends is the gigantic mobilization started by God, decreed and organized by him, so as to attack his own enemy. Countless hordes converge on the poor man. Where do they come from? Why do mighty armies assemble for the sole purpose of destroying one isolated adversary who cannot even defend himself? Why such a waste of military power?

The passages in which Job describes his position in the community show him to be alone, surrounded by a multitude of enemies. Here again we find the same *all against one*, but not in the same style. Faced with the formidable celestial armies, we hardly think of Job's ignoble persecutors, but the disproportion in numbers is the same and it is the same enemy. In both contexts, it can only be a matter of the same phenomenon.

All the characters are talking about the same violence . . . 'But that's impossible,' someone will protest. The grandiose, cosmic drama of the three friends cannot be reduced to the sordid persecution that Job denounces. Does not the divine vengeance unleash all the elements, the winds and storms, thunder and lightning, floods, droughts and savage beasts?

True, but let us look more closely. All these forces converge *simultaneously* on the enemy of God. The norms of verisimilitude may not be met, but as a result the *all against one* of the scapegoat mechanism stands out all the more clearly. It is the only organizing principle, but it controls everything. No matter who the adversaries are, their power relations remain the same. Behind the most monstrous, the least human and the least recognizable combatants, we can see the simple country people who gather against a single adversary – inevitably one of them, whom they have come to hate.

Along with the bands of warriors and the natural disasters are the creatures that are fighting for God. They gather around their victim to descend on him together, having come from the four corners of the universe. The same species reappear constantly in these bizarre tales: bulls, dogs, birds of prey, especially vultures. These vultures swarm around even the smallest carcass, forming a circle around him so as to share the spoils.

All these animals and many more can be found in myths. It is, of course, the most ferocious species that are chosen but also those that live in herds, those that hunt and attack collectively, or that feed together on carcasses: species that behave or seem to behave like men gathered against a common enemy – for example, when they participate in a manhunt.

There is always an allusion to the same basic theme: the destruction of a single victim by a host of enemies. The same violence is present, and it is this violence that must be examined if we are to understand the relationship between the two styles of discourse. Violence is the true 'referent'; barely disguised in the threats of the friends and not disguised at all in Job's laments. Although our two types of discourse seem so different, each deals, in its own way, with the same. They both refer to the process whereby a hero becomes a scapegoat; they both refer to the phenomenon of lynching – the first stages of which Job has already savoured.

Sacred discourses tend to 'elevate' the events related, which begin to look as if they occurred outside human history. Yet one can also see that the opposite is true. Look at the victim sweating in anguish, at the arrow that pierces his liver! In Job's more realistic description we rediscover such events, and the overlaps between the two discourses are never difficult to identify.

The multiplicity of enemies is always based on the same model, the human crowd. As divine vengeance begins its preparations, there is nothing in the universe that resists the growing 'turbulence' – taken in the sense of Michel Serres's discussion of the Latin *turba*.[1] Woe betide the person who is at the centre of this irresistible whirlwind, who lets himself be caught. The seething crowd is the perfect vehicle for divine vengeance. It hurls itself at the victim and tears him to pieces; all the participants share the same terrible appetite for violence. No one wishes to miss striking the final blow. The images of laceration and fragmentation remind us of the endless mythical and ritual dismemberments and the innumerable versions of the Dionysiac *diasparagmos*.

The *all against one* of collective violence is apparent even in the gathering of first three, then four men around Job, and even informs the structure of their speeches. The three, and then the four, form a smaller crowd within the larger one. The clumsy reinforcement brought by Elihu emphasizes the structure of impending death that dominates the book from beginning to end.

Words, too, form a crowd; countless, they swirl about the head of the victim, gathering to deliver the *coup de grâce*. The three series of speeches are like volleys of arrows aimed at the enemy of God. The accusations descend on Job like so many adversaries, intent upon the destruction of some friend. Their hostile speeches are not merely an image of collective violence, they are a form of active participation in it. Job is well aware of this, and denounces the verbal dismemberment to which he is subjected. The three friends crush him with their speeches, and pulverize him with words (19: 2).

Is it an exaggeration to associate these words with a lynching? The friends do not express themselves in gross insults, nor do they engage in physical brutalities. They do not spit on Job. After all, they are members of the elite. Is Job not guilty of gross exaggeration and overdramatization?

Absolutely not. By equating all the acts of violence against Job with services rendered to God, these speeches justify past brutalities and incite new ones. They are more formidable than any spitting. Their *performative* value is obvious.

The God of the friends hardly seems chivalrous – he never fights fairly, and pits as many as a thousand against a single enemy. Not very sporting of him, we may think, but this kind of ironic reaction is beside the point and rather outdated. It attacks religion abstractly and as a totality, without ever asking what lies behind its visions. For three centuries we have simply thought them to be imaginary. They are considered unimportant inventions, secondary to the appearance of a God whose strength lies in the number of those fighting beneath his banner.

The metaphysical God is believed to be the product of a primary metaphysical imagination, and the celestial armies are held to be secondary fabrications having relatively minor significance. I have always thought that the direction of this genesis should be reversed. We should start with these armies that are in no way celestial and therefore all the more real. We must begin with collective violence. And, for once, we do not have to postulate the violence or regard it as a simple hypothesis. The author confronts us with it at every occasion. It is all part of the persecution of which Job complains he is the victim.

The speeches of the friends reflect the sacred fury that takes hold of lynchers as the lynching draws near. From Dionysiac *mania* to Polynesian *amok*, there are a thousand different ways of indicating a collective trance that is also found in Greek tragedy. These inflammatory tirades are like those of the tragic chorus in the moments that precede the destruction of the victim, such as the murder of Pentheus in *The Bacchae* and the discovery of the 'culprit' in *Oedipus Rex*.

Under our very eyes, the three friends sacralize the violence. The insults and meanness are metamorphosed into the grandiose accomplishments of a supernatural mission. The celestial warriors are in fact everyone involved: neighbours from near and far, the affluent as well as the barefoot, the young and the old, long-time friends and close relatives – even Job's elderly wife, who says to him: 'Curse God, and die.'

How can we deny the relevance of collective persecution in primitive religion, in the face of these lengthy texts that alternate tirelessly between the laments of the persecuted and frantic calls for murder? The language is that of the sacred and of the most savage rituals in which the community prepares to share the body of the victim.

Whenever opinion turns against a leader formerly elevated by the people's favour, the community automatically attributes the change to the intervention of an absolute Justice. Thus a whole mythology of divine vengeance unfolds in the friends' speeches.

Since they are participating in his lynching, Job's friends do not understand that he is playing the role of scapegoat. Here the paradox of generative violence is revealed in a spectacular way. Those who create the sacred with their own violence are incapable of seeing its truth. This is what makes the friends totally deaf to the appeals Job is constantly making. The more they participate in violence against the unfortunate man, the more they are carried away by their own barbaric lyricism and the less they understand what they are doing.

The three friends are well aware of what the social order expects of them, but this knowledge in no way contradicts their basic ignorance about the scapegoat, their inability to understand Job's point of view. They have no idea of the moral reprobation the phenomenon inspires in Job and in the rest of us as well, thanks to the biblical text.

As the Gospels will say later of a similar affair, the three friends 'know not what they do' on the moral and religious plane. They know very well, on the other hand, what they should and should not do to someone whose punishment is a sacred task, to be accomplished with art. The meaning of this art may escape us, but it can always be recovered.

5

Realism and Transfiguration

When we finally acknowledge the real themes of the work and recognize their coherence, we rediscover the theory that was proposed in *Violence and the Sacred* and the works that followed.[1]

According to this theory, the unanimous violence of the group is transfigured into a sacred epiphany. In *The Bacchae* Pentheus becomes the epiphany of a revengeful Dionysus . . . In the Dialogues, the lynching of Job and of all 'wicked men' is identical to the intervention of divine vengeance . . .

For the crowd to perceive its own collective violence as sacred, it must exercise that violence unanimously against a victim whose innocence is no longer evident – and it is no longer evident as a result of this very unanimity. This is the message of *Violence and the Sacred*, and we have just observed precisely the same phenomenon.

Of the three friends, Bildad of Shuah seems to be most prone to mythology. He develops the theme of celestial armies into a mythology similar to that of the Greek Erinyes or the German Walkyries. Clearly the religion of Bildad and of his world has little to do with the manifestations of the biblical Yahweh, even those that are still most contaminated with mythological violence:

Disease devours his flesh,
    Death's First-Born gnaws his limbs.
He is torn from the shelter of his tent,
    and dragged before the King of Terrors.
The Lilith makes her home under his roof,
    while people scatter brimstone on his holding. (18: 13–15)

The *Jerusalem Bible* note on the passage reads as follows:

> The 'King of Terrors', a figure from oriental and Greek
> mythology (Nerga, Pluto, etc.), seems here to have infernal
> spirits (Furies) at command to plague the wicked man ever
> during his lifetime [. . .] Lilith, another figure of popular
> legend, is a female demon, [. . .] Brimstone produces, or
> is symbolic of sterility and is possibly (in this passage) a
> precaution against infection.

Not only the Indo-European but all the great mythological
systems contain these bands of supernatural killers who act
together unanimously and in so doing produce the sacred, and
sometimes even make their victims divine. This is the truly
mythological version of the celestial armies, also known as the
persecutors of Job.

Everything we have seen so far, or are about to see, fits the
arguments developed in my last three books.[2] If I failed to
mention this out of fear of being accused of 'reductionism' I
would not be able to carry out my intention of exploring the
vast regions of the Dialogues, nine-tenths of them in fact, that
are normally approached only by philologists. They are
avoided by biblical interpreters.

The Book of Job forces us to choose between the moral and
metaphysical analysis of the problem of evil, based on the one
hand on the reading contained in the prologue, and on the
other on the recognition of this formidable relationship between violence and the sacred, which is not consciously
articulated by the friends but is consciously rejected by the
scapegoat. The hypothesis of victimization allows the texts to
emerge from the silence that surrounds them and frees them
from the metaphysical and moral trap that prohibits their
interpretation. 'Reductionism', in this case, is a liberating
force in that it attacks this trap exclusively. The ordering
principle I apply to this considerable mass of data makes it
possible to read the texts independently of the system that has
constrained them.

The analysis of the Dialogues brings something new to my previous analyses. Not that it modifies in any way the conclusions I have already formulated – far from it. But it does show how the text, when analysed, forces us to draw these same conclusions for ourselves.

Once they have been freed from the prologue – and from now on that will be my assumption – the Dialogues present something particularly conclusive and convincing about the principles that govern the transformation of collective violence into the sacred.

It is sometimes argued that the scapegoat hypothesis cannot really be demonstrated, since it is never directly legible in a text. It describes a structuring process, and cannot be deduced directly from a single text. It is, in essence, comparative and hypothetical. I have said the same myself. As a matter of fact, with respect to the scapegoat mechanism all texts seem necessarily to belong to one of the following two categories:

1. Myths for which there is no direct proof that they are structured by the scapegoat mechanism; the very fact that they are implies that the mechanism is nowhere apparent. This is precisely what we observe in all the speeches that are not by Job. The friends cannot be expected to recognize their own injustice. As with all those who create scapegoats, they consider their victim to be guilty. Therefore, for them, there is no scapegoat.

2. Texts in which this same mechanism is revealed. The innocence of the victim is proclaimed; the scapegoat is clearly seen as such but the persecutors, by the same token, are no longer there to wax eloquent over divine vengeance and the celestial armies. They are no longer there to reveal for us the structuring effect that the process exercises on their language, their vision and their behaviour.

There is nothing more difficult than detecting the structuring mechanism at work in a text. It is like looking for depth on a two-dimensional surface, the written text.

To the extent that this impossibility can be overcome, the Dialogues overcome it. They are, precisely, dialogues in that they present the two visions in counterpoint. The true revelations of the persecuted alternate with the untruthful sacralized speeches of the persecutors.

Sometimes we do not even need this counterpoint. In some of the arguments I have quoted – those of Eliphaz for example, on 'the ancient trail trodden by the wicked', and those of Elihu on the God who crushes the great 'without inquiry' and on the crowd who tramples them – the scapegoating is so evident in the process of sacralization that we have no need to compare the two types of speech.

But sometimes there cannot be too much of a good thing. Of all the revelatory details offered by the Book of Job, the most extraordinary remains the counterpoint of the two perspectives, made possible by the dialogue format; it resembles a theatrical production, the object of which is not catharsis but the disappearance of all catharsis.

The correspondence between the two types of text cannot be considered a mere coincidence. Even if he cannot speak in our own language, even if he is sometimes out of his depth and taken aback by his own daring, the author manipulates these correspondences too skilfully not to be aware of them. The difference in perspective on the same act of collective violence is the true subject of the Dialogues. The sacred lie of the friends is contrasted with the true realism of Job.

6

Oedipus and Job

The counterpoint between the sacred and desacralizing discourses reveals a generalizable truth about all violent religions. It demystifies the traditional perspective not only on Job and the other scapegoats in his society, but on all the generative scapegoats of sacred violence.

Persecutors everywhere make their victims 'tread the ancient trail'. These journeys reach us only in the epics of divine vengeance, in the transfigured representations these epics offer of them. These are what we call myths.

Let us now apply Job's knowledge to the example of Oedipus. First we must compare the two stories. Even those who have compared them, such as Meyer Fortes in his *Oedipus and Job*,[1] have not perceived the extent of their similarity.

Popularity raised Oedipus even higher than Job, conferring on him the royal crown, which Job did not quite achieve. Suddenly, without warning, after an investigation that is so strange that it is more like Elihu's 'without inquiry', Oedipus is convicted of abominable crimes. His career collapses in the Terror so frequently evoked by Job's friends. With the same disconcerting rapidity, the idol is transformed into someone accursed, defiled, and stricken with plague. This man's collective punishment will restore the divine blessing temporarily withdrawn from the community because of its tardiness in mobilizing against the 'enemy of God'.

This mythological hero's career is too similar to Job's not to suggest the presence of the same phenomenon beneath the two texts: the transformation of a popular hero into a scapegoat.

It may be objected that although these similarities are real, parricide and incest amount to an irreducible difference between the two cases. Oedipus 'really' committed these crimes, and so cannot be the scapegoat for which I am always looking. The parricide and incest play a prominent role not only for Freud but for most modern critics, who are much more interested in these crimes than in Job's innocence.

What could have been the reason for the presence of these crimes in the myth? Supposedly, I am not asking the right question. The myth is of unknown origin: it is prudent to consider it totally fictitious. We will never know the origin of the parricide and incest, any more than we will know whether Thebes ever had a king by the name of Oedipus. We can get at these matters only by turning to psychoanalysis, to Freud and maybe even to Jung, but not otherwise. My efforts to inquire into the concrete origin of these themes by means of a *supposition* of a crowd phenomenon are thought to betray my naive realism. I disturb my contemporaries' keen sense of the uncertainty of everything.

But Job himself clearly suggests the very origin that I propose. When the crowd turns on him, it instigates all sorts of accusations but, in his case, they do not hold; they do not stick to Job; they are forgotten as fast as they are proposed.

Why? Because Job protests his innocence to the end. If his 'friends' had succeeded in reducing him to silence, the persecutors' belief in the scapegoat's guilt would have been unanimous. This belief would have prevailed so totally that every future account of the affair would have been given by people sharing it. We would have only one perspective, that of the friends. In other words, we would have a myth. That is all a myth is – an absolute faith in the victim's total power of evil that liberates the persecutors from reciprocal recriminations and, therefore, is identical with an absolute faith in the total power of good.

The accusations would be so powerful that they would be raised to the status of truth. They would be inseparable from Job and become a part of him. They would no longer even be recognized as accusations: whence the myth. Oedipus really did kill his father and marry his mother. He, not the community, is responsible for his shame and banishment. The friends say the same thing about Job, but we do not believe them because, in spite of everything, it is Job we believe. The victim has the last word in the Bible; we are influenced by this even though we do not want to pay the Bible the homage it deserves.

In Job's case, it is clear that the accusations increase *after* the crowd turns on its former idol, and therefore *because of that action.* If Job were not there to defend himself, our impression would be different. We would think that the crowd turned against Job after discovering his crime and, therefore, because of it. Such is the impression created by myth.

Admittedly the accusations are different, but again, if Job were not there to defend himself the accusations would quickly become as improbable and abusive as they are in the myth. When a crowd's hysteria can no longer be controlled, it almost always makes a pretext of parricide and incest.

There is something common to Job's ulcers and the plague that Oedipus is accused of spreading in Thebes. Like most great stories in the Bible, the Book of Job must originate in myth, a myth not very different from that of Oedipus; but whatever the myth, it has been mishandled by the more demanding and radical inspiration of the Jews.

The myth is Job's story told entirely by his persecutors. The Dialogues of Job are an Oedipus story in which the victim forever refuses to add his voice to those of his persecutors.

Oedipus is a *successful* scapegoat, because he is never recognized as such. Job is a *failed* scapegoat. He derails the mythology that is meant to envelop him, by maintaining his own point of view in the face of the formidable unanimity surrounding him. By remaining faithful to the truth revealed by the victim, Job is the true hero of knowledge rather than Oedipus, who is perceived as such in the philosophical tradition.

The victim must participate if there is to be perfect unanimity. His voice must be joined to the unanimous voice of condemnation. The perspective of the persecutors is transformed into indisputable truth by Oedipus' final submission to the imbecilic judgement of the crowd.

Oedipus is an expert in spontaneous confession, even before the time of psychoanalysis. He admits that he is accursed, evil and the enemy of God and that he deserves all the acts of vengeance that will be committed against him. Earlier the crowd had echoed the curse hurled at this future scapegoat in a language reminiscent of the inflamed tirades of the 'friends': the language of a manhunt made sacred and ritualized:

> Who is the man proclaimed
> by Delphi's prophetic rock
> as the bloody-handed murderer,
> the doer of deeds that none dare name?
> Now is the time for him to run
> with a stronger foot
> than Pegasus
> for the child of Zeus leaps in arms upon him
> with fire and the lightning bolt,
> and terribly close on his heels
> are the Fates that never miss.
>
> In the savage forests he lurks and in
> the caverns like
> the mountain bull.
> He is sad and lonely, and lonely his feet
> that carry him far from the navel of earth;
> but its prophecies, ever living,
> flutter around his head.[2]

The thesis that it is the sacrifice of a scapegoat that generates the religions of violence is simply obvious, and would have been known for centuries if so-called 'humanist' culture had not, since the Renaissance, closed itself off from the Bible's influence.

That influence has, however, been exerted in the domain of everyday reality, and often against those who pretend to speak in the name of the Bible. In *The Scapegoat* I pointed out the glaring homologies between the Oedipus themes and those found, before a lynching, among crowds delirious with mimesis. This occurs whenever the appetite for violence is combined with a heightened susceptibility to the mimetic contagion and substitution that produce a unanimous scapegoat.

We now know how these themes originate, and every time they are reported as truth we recognize them immediately as the reflection of the mentality of persecution. For example, no one is deceived any longer by the accusations of incest or infanticide made against the Jews during the Black Death in order to 'convince' them that they were the cause of the plague.

Acts of collective violence may very well be real when the accusations are as stereotypically fantastic as in the myth of Oedipus. Why would the result be different in the two cases? We know that these themes do not originate in a context of purely poetic fantasy; their conjunction is never innocent and, in the case of Oedipus, it is all the more suggestive in that it destroys the brilliant career of a parvenu.

My analysis of Oedipus, in the light of Job, fits perfectly with the analysis I made within the framework of historical persecutions. In fact, the analysis is always the same. Although the Bible is little appreciated by the modern sensibility, its message is sufficiently understood for us to have the sole ability to prevent future mythical crystallizations by recognizing that they are only the illusions of persecutors.

It may very well be that the history of the French Revolution is mythical in a broad sense, but it is never mythical enough to present itself to us in the form of a new myth of Oedipus. Yet we can very well see the possible germs of this myth in the most obvious cases of the mentality of persecution. If that mentality had become universal, we could easily imagine a fusion of two persons in one – the young Louis XVII, accused of incest with his mother, and Philippe Egalité, casting the vote for the death of the king at the Convention.

Nothing else is needed to reconstruct the Oedipus who committed incest and parricide.

This sort of mythological crystallization is not possible in
our universe. We can immediately see it for what it is. But this
ability of ours comes to a complete halt, having been literally
prohibited at the threshold of 'high culture'. We have not
transported it into worlds that are foreign to us, particularly
the 'classical' world. Any new mythological crystallization is
smothered at birth, but we have not been successful in un-
ravelling those inherited by the ethnologists or ennobled by
literature. The Bible has given us the privileged tool of demystification, but we either do not know how to use it, or do
not want to use it. Perhaps we are secretly afraid it will wreak
too much havoc.

Our scholars think they 'don't believe in myths' because
they are wholly fictive, but their own unquestioning
acceptance of parricide and incest is a belief that perpetuates
the illusion of persecution, which is the essence of mythical
illusion.

Pious classicists constantly hark back to the famous fatality
that eliminates any inquiry into mythological accusations and
makes the tragic hero an unconscious criminal whose crime is
fully documented, although unknown to himself. Like Job's
friends, the critics constantly rely on the example of Oedipus
and shake their heads sententiously.

The idea that myth is totally fictional makes it as im-
penetrable as its opposite, religion, which accepts it as truth.
The humanists' scepticism seems to be the ultimate criticism
of religion yet, in reality, it is its heir and, like all heirs, is only
too interested in the perpetuation of the capital to be inherited
not to respect it secretly. Under conditions radically changed
by biblical revelation, the humanists' scepticism prevents the
revelation of the role played by the scapegoat mechanism in
the genesis and organization of myths. This scepticism
partakes in the continuation of scapegoat religions because it
protects their secret.

The parallel between Oedipus and Job reveals the superiority of the biblical text, for the Bible achieves a truly radical demystification, a demystification that amounts to the resolution of the enigma that mythology presents for us.

There is, indeed, a tragic demystification and I am not denying what I said in *Violence and the Sacred*. This tragic demystification emphasizes and extracts many of the resemblances between Oedipus and Job, but it cannot cross a certain threshold that the biblical text crosses.

The tragic action is a struggle between the protagonists for influence over the people – a mimetic rivalry, exactly as in Job. Oedipus finally loses in a contest that he might have won. All this is strongly suggested by one tragic author, Sophocles, who minimizes the parricide and incest for as long as possible. But Sophocles takes them up again at the end of the 'ancient trail', so as not to change the ritual itinerary. Sophocles does not directly challenge the religious beliefs of the Greek counterparts of Eliphaz.

Tragic demystification is a mere sketch or suggestion beside that of Job. Like Job, Oedipus at first vigorously resists the accusations made against him. He shrugs his shoulders at the first mention of parricide, but he yields in the end and his submission is disguised as a startling confirmation of the two crimes. It appears to verify the oracles, supported by a single witness who neither denies nor confirms the persistent rumour that Laius was assassinated not by *one* but by *several* murderers.

After repeating five or six times during his search that he must clear up this rumour, Oedipus never asks the question he has been turning over in his mind. He gives up the struggle and turns all his attention to accusing himself of everything the people want. This business of *many murderers* refers vaguely to the collective violence concealed by the oracles, while contributing to it by calling for new victims. The many murderers of Laius provide an example of collective violence, and collective violence is about to deal with the overly curious Oedipus.

How can we overlook an allusion to the pattern of

victimization in a text that is entirely immersed in undeniable allusions to the role of scapegoat, a role that Oedipus finally plays in total conformity to the traditional scenario?

In the first scene the king says to the Thebans, who had come to beg him to cure them: 'I know you are all sick, yet there is not one of you, sick though you are, that is as sick as I myself. My spirit groans for the city and myself and you at once.'

Just before the shepherd's arrival, Oedipus and Jocasta recall once more the rumour of *many* murderers, and Oedipus exclaims: 'You said that he spoke of highway *robbers* who killed Laius. Now if he uses the same number, it was not I who killed him. One man cannot be the same as many.' This sentence echoes the preceding one, which it contradicts. By accepting royalty every man runs the risk of becoming a scapegoat, and Oedipus implicitly recognizes this in his first sentence. When his time comes, Oedipus first tries to hide but finally has to submit.

Sophocles demonstrates his keen insight here but it does not prevent him, also, at the end of *Oedipus Rex* from giving in and becoming the consenting dupe of this myth; yet he is not unaware of its fictitious character containing the falsehood of persecution. I am indebted to Sandor Goodhart's studies for this entire analysis.[3]

7

'Jezebel Trampled to Death under the Horses' Hooves'

In *The Poetics* Aristotle clearly set the limits of tragic demystification by forbidding dramatists to be too radical in the changes they make in their adaptations of legends. People know these stories by heart; they could be angered if the poet were to make too many changes, especially if the public were, thereby, deprived of the spectacular chastisement of a victim.

Without this substitute for sacrificial immolation that readers expect of the poet, they may well turn on him and obtain that *catharsis* at his expense as if to prove, by this regression, the violent origins of all tragic theatre.

According to one significant legend, Euripides ended his days devoured by dogs who resembled closely the killer animals mentioned by Job's friends or those of Queen Jezebel in the Book of Kings. They are the same dogs, the same horses, the very same beasts everywhere, the same *diasparagmos*:

Trampled to death under the horses' hooves,
The mangled members of her hideous corpse
Left to the dogs that came to lap her blood?[1]

The poet of *Athaliah* also did not fail to include these dogs. Nor did he omit Orestes' serpents, nor the horses that are even more responsible than the monster for the death of their master, Hippolytus, in *Phaedra*. Permit me to digress on Racine, although it is not entirely a digression.

Racine never misses the opportunity to develop wisely, and at length, all that mythological and historical sources provide in the way of collective and sacrificial violence. He is careful to preserve their religious significance: the death of Pyrrhus in a temple, at the foot of the sacrificial altar; Iphigenia – or rather Eriphile, the difference is unimportant – sacrificed by the entire Greek army; Aman, at the end of *Esther*, thrown to the crowd who tears him apart; in *Athaliah*, the queen's death is naturally the same as her mother's. By giving us Athaliah's dream, Racine lets us know that he, too, is very familiar with 'the ancient trail trodden by the wicked'. In his book *Sur Racine*, Roland Barthes perceived the fundamental role of collective murder. He clearly understood it, since he recognized in the famous scene of the father of the primitive horde (*Totem and Taboo*) the common denominator of all Racine's intrigues. Yet to hark back to Freud in this manner reflects a timidity that limits somewhat the significance of these remarks.

There is no true tragedy in which the hero does not follow the famous 'trail' to the final climax of terror. And if the sources provide nothing on this level, Racine is perfectly capable of inventing the collective murder necessary for his conclusions.

One might think there is no place for such a murder in *Britannicus*. Neither Tacitus' account nor the nature of the imperial order authorizes a conclusion in the style of *The Bacchae*: the dismemberment of a victim by the crowd, the *diasparagmos* of a scapegoat. Yet June flees the imperial palace. On the way, she meets a statue of the divine Augustus. She bathes its feet with tears; she holds it in a tight embrace. The people are moved and take the virgin under their protection. Nero does not dare to make a move, but the diabolical Narcissus hurls himself into pursuit of his prey:

Narcissus, bolder, and intent to please,
Makes for fair June, and unabashed begins
To stop her in her flight with impious hand.
This recklessness is punished by a hail
Of deadly blows. His blood spurts out on June.
Caesar, struck by so many sights at once,
Abandons him to his avengers' hands.[2]

Racine invents a collective murder in all his plays wherever none is provided by the Roman sources. Although June's purity seems to predate this sacrifice, in reality it stems from the blood of the victim spilling over her. This purity acquires a religious significance; it becomes that of the vestal virgin.

This first scene is identical with the scene of Hippolytus' death that follows. In the case of Hippolytus, the angry people are the horses who revolt against their master and, before killing him, drag him to the edge of a sacred place where Aricia is waiting. Flesh is always torn apart, if not on the sacrificial altar then at least beside it, and the blood always gushes over the survivor in order to revive or, rather, create the virgin harmony of post-sacrificial dawns:

> I watched, my lord, I watched
> Your helpless son dragging behind the steeds
> His hands had fed. He tried to call to them:
> Instead, his cries startle them. So they gallop
> And make one wound of all his living flesh.
> Now as the plain is pealing with our grief
> The violent fit is spent. They slacken speed,
> And stop, where close at hand his father's tombs
> And ancient sculptures hold the chill remains
> And memories of Kings.[3]

Racine perceives and reproduces the role of the animal in mythological murder. For the murder of Jezebel, which prophesies the murder of Athaliah, devouring dogs are not sufficient, so he brings back the horses of Hippolytus. 'Trampled to death under the horses' hooves.' It is unimportant whether Racine's endings are taken entirely, partially, or not at all from other sources. In a sense they are never his own imaginings. He always demonstrates the same control in dealing with violence and the sacred and it is always a matter, above all else, of collective murder.

It is in this that the famous imitation of ancient writers consists. Among the greatest writers, this imitation is an exact understanding of what is required for the sacrificial function of tragedy. Whether pure invention or the closest imitation, the result is always in strict conformity with the great models bequeathed by the tragedies closest to the sacrificial origin.

An ending in the form of collective murder would seem improbable in the most cloistered and confined of Racine's tragedies, *Bajazet*, in which the crowd is inevitably most absent. Yet it contains another dream, another nightmare with the same theme as the Dream of Athaliah. Rather than a real dream, it is the madness of Orestes beginning again. The unfortunate Atalide finds herself pursued not only by the person whom she accuses herself of having lost but by all those who loved Bajazet, all his friends, relatives and ancestors, transformed into a troop of vengeful Erinyes. We are reminded of the celestial armies of the 'friends' who hurl themselves on their victim. Here are the final lines of the play:

> Oh, have I loved thee but to murder thee?
> Nay, I can bear it not. My hand forthwith
> Must punish me, take vengeance for thy death.
> Ye whose rest I did vex, whose honour stain,
> Heroes who should in him have lived again,
> Unhappy mother, who long ere we grew up
> Gave me his heart with a far different hope,
> Luckless vizier, his friends now desperate,
> Roxana – come ye all, banded in hate,
> To torture a distracted woman's heart!
> Take your revenge: that is her just desert. [She stabs
> herself][4]

Atalide brings about the transfiguration of her own suicide into collective murder – or rather, these lines bring out the true meaning of all suicide: the total absence of succour, universal hostility, the dark side of the unanimity of persecution. This same profound sense of suicide reappears in Phaedra, who feels expelled from heaven, earth and hell all at the same time. Admittedly, this feeling could be the result of fantasy, especially in the paranoiac aspects of modern man. But does it always result from it, necessarily and from the beginning?

Is not collective persecution always an illusion of our abused senses? Do victims really exist? What is the difference between the abuses of psychiatric analysis and an effective denial of the very real horrors of history? What is really projected in all the 'projections of persecution' and the 'hallucinations of a dismembered body'?

I am not attempting to determine who was the most perceptive – Racine, Sophocles, or any of the tragic writers, or the author of the Dialogues. That would be ridiculous. Sophocles certainly did not share our *précieux* illusions about myths, nor did Racine, but their knowledge remains ambiguous and ultimately sterile, a process of allusions that remains somewhat esoteric.

Even though he does not take the accusations of the myth seriously, Sophocles suggests that Oedipus, in his arrogant and unwise inquiry, has done everything to provoke the disaster that overwhelms him. The critics are clearly aware of Sophocles' attitude, but do not draw the appropriate conclusions. They do not perceive that it implies an extreme scepticism towards the real concept of the myth: that the plague of Thebes was actually caused by parricide and incest.

Oedipus was the first to become involved in the search for a scapegoat and his bad example turns against him. Thanks to his ultimate docility the tragedy comes to a harmonious end, so well achieved that almost no one is aware that it represents a system of scapegoat illusion.

Even though the author perceives the injustice of the scapegoating process, he does not adopt the victim's perspective. Sophocles seems to be saying two things: 'Stories of parricide and incest are nonsense, but it was Oedipus who stirred up the hornet's nest. He was playing with fire and got burned. It is not my job to extricate him.' This indifference towards the victim's role as victim does not only have moral consequences. It prevents the myth from disintegrating.

Job is quite a different question. Job is unthinkable for the Greeks and their modern successors. Imagine an unyielding Oedipus who scoffs at fate, and especially at parricide and incest; who persists in treating oracles as sinister traps for scapegoats, which is what they unquestionably are. He would have the whole world against him – Hellenists, Heidegger, Freud and all the academics. He would have to be killed on the spot or put away in a psychiatric ward for insuperable repression.

All this would hardly have helped Western civilization and its literature. Catharsis would lose its efficacy and all forms of the sublime would decompose. The great form of tragedy, the highest of all forms, would lose its balance. It would forfeit its acceptable conclusion. We see this clearly today in the demise of that form. The sacrificial subterfuges are exhausted. But it has taken a long time to reach this stage.

A quick glance at the Book of Job is sufficient to understand the scorn for the literature of the Bible. It is full of repetitions and frayed all over. Only the false prologue and conclusion provide a semblance of unity to the chaos. Decidedly, they are both as indispensable to the aesthete as to the moralist and metaphysician. Without them, we would no longer find ourselves confronted with

> A mass of mangled flesh and bone, and slime,
> And tatters rolled in blood, and ghastly limbs
> Fought over by the dogs that fed on them.[5]

III
MIMESIS

8

'A Whole Country Possessed by Saint Vitus's Dance'[1]

One essential dimension of the scapegoat thesis remains to be traced: mimesis. All the conditions for its presence seem to be assembled here. The vanished prestige of Job seems to have been a personal acquisition. Apparently it did not come with any of Job's functions, nor did he inherit it. From the pleasure it gave him, we can assume that he had not always possessed it. He is a man who has risen from the ranks.

What was his status? Probably very high, but Job was not the only one to occupy it. Obviously he was a man of property, as were his three 'friends' Eliphaz of Teman, Bildad of Shuah and Zophar of Naamath, and others equally. We are among members of an elite who dominated local political life. The most enterprising of the members sought to increase their power by currying popular favour. Job was the most successful of them all; then, suddenly, he lost everything. Why?

For Job to have been the object of such extravagant flattery and veneration before becoming the scapegoat it was no doubt sufficient, given the fickleness of the society, for him to have had one early success that made him *primus inter pares*. The desires of the people of his class were polarized on that first difference, which they magnified out of all proportion. It was the elite who chose him, in the first place, for their model and flattered, venerated and imitated him slavishly. The rest of the people then followed, imitating his first imitators.

Proof of this adulation among friends can be found precisely in the title 'friends' that no one denies, even though they behave like Job's enemies. Should we believe that a real friendship or intimacy exists among them? There is no indication of this. The three are 'friends' in the way that anyone in our own society can call himself the friend of a famous person. This friendship is merely another name for the boot-licking described in Chapter 29.

The absence of social distance encourages reciprocal imitation among equals. Job becomes identified with his success, so that to desire the same success is to desire Job himself, the incomparable being of Job. This identification is eminently competitive, and therefore ambivalent from the outset. Among his own class, Job has only rivals who are trying to outstrip him. They all want to become the same sort of uncrowned king that he was.

But royalty, by its very definition, cannot be shared. Job cannot possibly succeed in this way without provoking enormous jealousy around him. He is the *obstacle model* of mimetic theory. He stirs up Nietzschean resentment; the undertow of admiration always ends in a disastrous encounter with the obstacle which the model has become. Precisely because it is rooted in mimetic desire, the fascination roused by this too-fortunate rival has a tendency to become implacable hatred, a hatred that it already contains within itself. The type of fascination, full of hatred, that is apparent in almost all the speeches of the 'friends' thrives among men who are social equals.

Although the friends, like Job, evoke his past glory, it is not for the same reason but rather, spitefully and ironically, to teach him a lesson. They feed on the contrast between present and past. Their envy must have been enormous to continue to exist after their idol's downfall. They remind Job of the change in his fortune with a somewhat obscene liveliness; in a way, they are confirming their own happiness:

> If one should address a word to you, will you
>   endure it?
>   Yet who can keep silent?
> Many another, once, you schooled,
>   giving strength to feeble hands;
>   your words set right whoever wavered,
>   and strengthened every failing knee.
> And now your turn has come, and you lose patience too;
>   now it touches you, and you are overwhelmed. (4: 2–5)

Without men's tendency to imitate each other's desires, envy would not be so extraordinarily powerful in human society. Envy is merely the reciprocal borrowing of desires, under conditions of sufficient equality to ensure the development of mimetic rivalries.

The envy of 'friends' and their neighbours is essential to the transition from the first mimetic unanimity to the second. Equality of conditions sharpens the basic duplicity of the mimetic reactions inspired by the 'great man'. But even if imitation and desire are modulated differently at different social levels, ultimately both are found at all levels, and the frustration of the model obstacle is universal. There is never any essential difference between the friends and the rest of the people.

The feedback of the rivalry and the reciprocal retroaction of model and obstacle intensify the frustration that is finally satisfied by substitute victims, identified mimetically for lack of being able to achieve its end directly. But there is no fundamental difference between the mimesis of sacrificial sub-stitution and the mimesis of the friends' envy. The crowd merely follows upon and amplifies the successive reactions of the elite, and to a certain degree, the reverse is true as well.

Envy can exist only between Job and his equals, but within that situation its existence is more than likely. After a period of positive imitation, there must have been, among Job's 'natural' rivals, a hidden growth of envy that waited for direct expression until his first mistake, some incident that could be cleverly exploited to ruin Job's popularity among the people.

Watched on all sides, the idol runs the risk of being trans-formed into a scapegoat as a result of the slightest mistake. The mimesis of envy and hatred spreads as rapidly as the mimesis of admiration. It is the same mimesis that is trans-muted when the model becomes obstacle, a mimesis *scandalized* by this metamorphosis.

Among the lower ranks of society, noone could rival Job personally, but everybody was oppressed enough to accept blindly, mimetically, the scapegoats suggested to them, the enemies of those who oppress them. Thus they can satisfy their permanent bitterness on the most desirable and prestigious victims who, just yesterday, were all-powerful.

Job's decline in public opinion had to have begun in his own social circle and then spread downwards. The untouchables of Chapter 30 would never dare attack Job as they do without the encouragement of the upper class. This is hardly conjecture: the friends' speeches incite popular violence.

There must, therefore, be a certain time-lag between the reactions of the elite and those of the crowd. This interim permits the interpretation of an important theme which I have not yet mentioned, even though it is present in the speech of Eliphaz on 'the ancient trail trodden by the wicked'. It is the theme of *delayed* divine vengeance.

Although they are already his declared enemies, God still heaps his benefits on the 'wicked' men. What is the reason for this prolonged divine kindness? Again, it is too easy to consider the theme 'purely' imaginary on the pretext that it is religious. We can deduce from preceding observations what is real in the motif of divine favour being bestowed too long on the wicked.

This interim during which the wicked and the accursed enjoy divine favour lasts as long as is necessary to bring the 'Just' to the edge of despair. What does that mean? Why does God take his time in destroying his enemies? Could he be their dupe? That is impossible. The classic response embedded in scapegoat religion is that God, far from being duped, is resorting to strategy. He is setting a diabolical trap for those who rebel against him. He encourages an arrogance on their part that will ultimately be fatal for them.

In itself, this response implies the crowd's participation in divine vengeance. The longer divine favours dwell on the wicked, the greater their arrogance becomes. God does not cultivate this arrogance because he needs it to judge the wickedness of the wicked. The trap he sets for them proves that he has already condemned them.

The arrogance of the wicked does not enlighten God, but

rather the people who are swayed by their leaders' charm. It stirs legitimate envy and resentment among many men. It facilitates the general mobilization of the celestial armies. If God had undertaken to settle the affair by himself, all this manoeuvring would have been useless. Once more he uses as intermediary a crowd that has shown great patience but finally shakes off its lethargy when faced with the excesses of those who had succeeded in winning its favour.

God delays his intervention in order for the fall of the wicked to be as spectacular and cruel as possible. If the sadistic concept of the divine implied by it is unacceptable to us, then we must interpret the idea of *delayed* vengeance as a function of the envious sentiments we sense in the friends of Job.

The less fortunate rivals of the powerful become impatient with the relative stability of a power that, for them, must be contrary to the divine will, since it offends them. They would like to hasten the probable course of things, but they dare not openly oppose those whom the populace still venerates.

If Job had reason to believe that men like Eliphaz, Bildad and Zophar could replace him as scapegoat, then that would mean they could also replace him as the idol of the people, and perhaps their chance will come after his downfall. This same possibility from which Job has excluded them is precisely what made them his untiring opponents. They felt oppressed by him; they may really have been oppressed, but primarily they were humiliated. The fundamental emotion is mimetic rivalry, envy inspired by a too-successful rival. In this instance, that envy is masked by the fierce God of an immemorial tradition.

Job is perfectly aware that the scapegoat is interchangeable with those who persecute him most fiercely, his so-called friends. He imagines the situation reversed, in order to show that suffering alone makes the only true difference:

I too could talk like you,
   were your soul in the plight of mine.
I too could overwhelm you with sermons,
   I could shake my head over you,
and speak words of encouragement,
    until my lips grew tired.
But, while I am speaking, my suffering remains. (16: 4–6)

Great men are too popular to succumb immediately to the intrigues that proliferate around them. Mimetic rivalry broods a long time in the shadows. That, for me, is the significance of the 'delay' in divine vengeance. Opinion wearies of its idols; it ends in destroying what it adored, in the forgetting of its own adoration. This is the triumph of the 'friends', and it is at this moment that the Dialogues take place.

9

Psalm 73

My argument is somewhat conjectural in that the envy directed towards Job is not explicit. The friends themselves, of course, do not mention it. Job only alludes to it. The text that links mimetic envy directly to the phenomenon of the sacralized scapegoat is not to be found in Job. But it is found elsewhere in the Bible, in Psalm 73, which is both very similar and very different from those I have quoted, very similar in subject matter and very different in perspective.

The narrator presents himself as a Righteous man, a faithful follower of the true God, who has long been discouraged by the apparent inertia of divine Justice. He specifically mentions the envy inspired by the brilliant career of those whom he considers ungodly. Fortunately, God finally decided to intervene.

Contrary to other tragic psalms that were written from the victim's point of view, this is one of the rare psalms that reflects the other perspective, that of the 'friends'. In fact it is the only one about which we can state, categorically, that it reflects the perspective of the persecutors:

My feet were on the point of stumbling,
a little further and I should have slipped,
envying the arrogant as I did,
and watching the wicked get rich.

For them, no such thing as pain,
their bodies are healthy and strong,
they do not suffer as other men do,
no human afflictions for them!

So pride is their chain of honour,
violence the garment that covers them;
their spite oozes like fat,
their hearts drip with slyness.

Cynical advocates of evil,
lofty advocates of force,
they think their mouth is heaven
and their tongue can dictate on earth.

This is why my people turn to them
and lap up all they say, [. . .]

until the day I pierced the mystery
and saw the end in store for them:
they are on a slippery slope, you put them there,
you urge them on to ruin,

until suddenly they fall,
done for, terrified to death.

The individual who is speaking has long been fretting over a group of men who have been very popular but whose flashy success has suddenly ended in terror. Again we encounter 'the ancient trail'. These people have trodden it to the very edge of the abyss, and if a list of the 'Wicked' existed, their names would appear on it beside that of Job.

The narrator rejoices at the sight of a disaster similar to the one that strikes Job. He approves and becomes the accomplice of an act of collective violence which he thinks is divine. He helps us to imagine the intimate thoughts of Job's enemies, the thoughts that his three friends keep to themselves.

Proof that the infatuation of the people is the essential factor in the episode can be found in the phrase 'my people turn to them'. From the narrator's perspective, the people assure the success of men who ought not to succeed but do so nevertheless, and their abuse of power continues as long as they enjoy the favour of the people.

The long-lasting career of the 'Wicked' brings despair to the

'Righteous' and rouses in him an envy that, in this case, is apparent in everything he writes. His envy is so strong that this Righteous man is almost ready to give up his objections and follow the example of the Wicked, even possibly pay court to them, like everybody else.

Fortunately, the Righteous man holds fast. The downfall of the Wicked occurs just in time to re-establish the credibility of eternal justice and to deliver the envious from his envy. What he mistook for divine inertia is a wise delay. The Righteous man had not understood that it was a question of divine strategy:

> until the day I pierced the mystery
> and saw the end in store for them:
> they are on a slippery slope, you put them there,
> you urge them on to ruin,

The final downfall of the Wicked is seen as a double victory, for God and for the Righteous man who has suffered humiliation for so long. Admittedly, the overthrow took a long time, but one should never despair. Public opinion remains faithful to its favourites for a long time, much longer than their jealous rivals would wish, but finally it shakes off its torpor and settles its account with the accursed.

When a man is raised above us and makes our lives intolerable, probably he is making the lives of quite a few others intolerable also. We can therefore expect that sooner or later public opinion will change and set its mechanism in motion. The longer this takes, the slower and even more dubious divine justice appears, but ultimately it will regain its reputation of infallibility.

The Righteous man is very clear about the element of envy in his positive imitation, but when that envy becomes more intense as a result of the obstacle – the scandal – of the triumph of the 'Wicked', this imitation turns to hatred and is no longer recognized as such by the Righteous.

Yet if any envy is worthy of the name, this is it. In the

moment of crisis, the Righteous man does not recognize that his counter-imitation, his extreme resentment, is a result of his envy. He sees it as the very best of sentiments, religious fervour at its purest. There is only one unique element of mystification left, but it is the most important, for he resembles the friends whose extreme envy becomes religious hysteria.

Psalm 73 is not in the highest tradition of biblical inspiration in which the voice of the victim is heard. It is similar to that of the friends in the Book of Job. The highest inspiration – and the only inspiration that is specifically biblical – is that of Job, the only one that has no real equivalent in the Greek world or elsewhere.

This text, nevertheless, deserves its place in the collection of psalms that deal with collective victims. This becomes very clear when we compare its role to that of Job's interrogators. If the Bible simply gave the monopoly of words to the victim instead of to the persecutors – if it substituted, as Nietzsche claims, a slave morality for that of the master – the revelation would be much less powerful, both on the moral and intellectual planes, which are really one. We would not be constantly asked to confront both perspectives. The Bible would merely be the revenge (symbolic or real) implied in Nietzsche's qualification of the biblical process. It would be reduced to a process of mimetic doubles, an inversion of signs without any essential significance. This is far from being the case.

Very similar arguments to those of Psalm 73 can be found in Greek tragedy. The chorus is indignant over the success of the arrogant, and there is a temptation to scepticism and impiety, inspired by divine action. Why serve the gods if *hybris* goes unpunished? Fortunately, *hybris* is always ultimately punished. Too rapid a rise is always paid for by as sudden a downfall. Aeschylus, Sophocles, Euripides all comment on the reciprocal affinity of extreme heights and depths. The chorus celebrates its own mediocrity, which it considers a reassurance. Extraordinary fortunes attract divine punishment.

The violent succession of *tyrants* corresponds to the 'ancient trail of the wicked'. We sense an instability whose political dimension is obvious and essential, but interpretations limited to it are distorted by the interpreter's tendency to favour either the tyrant or, more often, the crowd. By injecting anachronistic meanings into these matters, by taking sides, we inevitably ignore the true centre of gravity of the process – the scapegoat mechanism, still religiously transfigured, at least up to a point. The whole religious dimension of these events remains hidden by too exclusive an emphasis on the political aspects, real as they are.

Primitive religion is never idle. In our ignorance, we think of it as 'pure and simple' superstition. But to perceive its truth, we have to disentangle the hidden 'paradoxes' of mimetic desire, transfigured by the sacralization in which they are couched.

By recognizing the role played by the hysterical crowd in religions of violence we can separate the wheat from the tares and make use of the reality of what is hidden by the language of the sacred, without any fear of becoming its dupe.

Like Greek tragedy the Prophets, the Diaologues of Job, and the Psalms reflect great political and social crises that are also religious. These crises all contribute to the decadence of the sacrificial systems that were still in use in the two societies. We are at that junction between religion which is still sacrificial in the strict sense, and politics that is *sacrificial* in the broad sense. Certain aspects of the religious speech can already be translated into a political speech, and vice versa.

Thanks to the work of the *CREA*[1] and others, our knowledge of this ambiguous field is rapidly increasing, but its development will be so disturbing for the social sciences that we can anticipate strong resistance.

10

The Mountain Torrent

The conditions favourable to all mimetic phenomena are clearly present in the Dialogues. Imitation which is at first positive and later negative, combined with the imitative resentment spread by the friends and people like them, perfectly accounts for the two successive unanimities and the order of their succession, first *around* Job, and then *against* him.

Are there explicit references in the Dialogues to this double mimesis? This would appear to be asking too much of an author who is neither a philosopher nor a theoretician and who does not have at his disposal an adequate language for discussing such things. Yet it is always the philosophers and theoreticians who do not perceive mimetic desire, whereas the poets are aware of it.

The Dialogues are no exception. Mimetic desire is revealed in a great metaphor that expresses equally both the diachronic complexity of the relationships created and their sychronic uniformity and essential impoverishment. A more simple and luminous equivalent of what Eric Gans would call the 'paradox' of these relationships[1] cannot be imagined:

> My brothers have been fickle as a torrent,
>   as the course of a seasonal stream.
> Ice is the food of their dark waters,
>   they swell with the thawing of the snow;
> but in the hot season they dry up,
>   with summer's heat they vanish.

Caravans leave the trail to find them,
  go deep into desert, and are lost.
The caravans of Tema look to them,
  and on them Sheba's convoys build their hopes.
Their trust proves vain,
  they reach them only to be thwarted. (6: 15–20)

Streams, in a semi-desert climate, never provide what men want. They are glutted when the snows melt and water is plentiful, but there is only sand for the rest of the year, which is dominated by thirst.

At the time when everyone was paying court to Job, false friends were constantly offering their services. Now that Job has need of support, everyone is in hiding. Like water in the heat of the sun, the goodwill has evaporated.

We expect true friends to support us in adversity, when the rest of the world is hostile towards us. And when we are surrounded with vile flatterers, we expect an extreme wariness on their part. True friendship demands a spirit of independence and courage.

Only a very strong resistance to mimetic contagion can safeguard that independence. All mimetic sentiments are of a kind. Stupid fads of fashion result in the fierce exclusion of scapegoats. Immunity to mimesis is a very rare and precious quality.

Far from possessing such a virtue the friends, like everyone else, are always drawn in the direction of the strongest mimetic attraction. On every occasion they are detrimental to Job's interests. They can never be counted on; for them to behave tomorrow as they behaved today, the crowd must also be constant.

Job understands the situation very clearly. 'I shall not find a single sage among you', he cries out in despair (17: 10). The same people who stir up popular hatred for Job used to elbow their way to the front of the flatterers. We think they have changed, but the change is part of their mimetic nature. It is the opposite of freedom. They are merely particles of the crowd.

Job says: 'My brothers have been fickle as a torrent' (6: 15). To whom, precisely, does this metaphor apply? If the word 'brothers' merely indicates the three friends, Job's interrogators, the metaphor would not be pertinent. It must apply to the whole community, which is hardly distinguishable from the friends. Today it is raining, and the friends are so many drops of water among countless others. If tomorrow the sun is shining, they will be the grains of sand in the burning desert.

The two unanimities that make of Job alternately an idol and a scapegoat correspond to the spring flood and the total drought. If the three friends were not always subject to the fashion of the moment, like everyone else, there would be no unanimity.

Their mimesis makes these three completely *representative* of a community that is itself mimetic. If all the citizens were present around Job, we would learn no more than we know already. The three comrades suffice for everyone, like the chorus in Greek tragedy.

The metaphor of the torrent not only indicates the absence of what is most desirable – whatever that may be – but also the superabundant, overwhelming presence of the undesirable – whatever, equally, that may be. The accursed stream eventually always brings us what it has made us desire by depriving us of it, but at the very moment it brings it, we no longer desire it; we even avoid it like the plague, so that from now on it is the plague.

What was unobtainable yesterday should cease to be unobtainable only by appearing in reasonable amounts. Instead, it can be found everywhere – it invades, submerges, and supplants everything *ad nauseam*. We are overwhelmed. We think we are stuck with it for ever, and we are, for a season. We wish it to the devil.

This absence of moderation, the perpetual combination of lack and excess, characterizes a universe that has surrendered to mimeticism. Rivalry is such a natural result of the imitation of desires that mimesis comes to regard the triumphant rival as indispensable. The obstacle supersedes the model. The model is chosen for its function as obstacle. If nothing thwarts it, mimetic masochism ceases to desire. There is no longer a model worthy of imitating.

Desire seeks out a 'better' obstacle: one that is more resistant, more insuperable. It always finds one. And that which no longer interests it immediately, in its turn, becomes interested. Other imitators are also in search of an obstacle. Only indifference can attract and engage them for any length of time, for it constitutes the insuperable obstacle. On the market of desire, any supply that is the object of a demand dries up instantly, and if the demand is exhausted, the supply proliferates monstrously.

Desire is far from pleased with anything that appears welcoming and agreeable. Whereas everything elusive attracts it, everything that rejects it is seductive. Without knowing it, it digs the bed of this torrent that always betrays it. Desire imagines the world in terms of this absurd division between desirable and non-desirable.

What is diabolical about the torrent is its cyclical nature – the promise it keeps, but always too late, of providing men with what they are deprived of all year long. By periodically reversing its gifts and its refusals, it perpetually keeps alive unsatisfied desires. The streams needed urgently by the caravans were too abundant yesterday not to make it unbelievable that they would have already disappeared at the first moment that they are needed.

With no break in continuity, the metaphor draws from that single torrent both the actions of normal desire and those that lead to death. It eliminates simply and elegantly the mistaken common-sense notion that claims there must be at least two causes of such apparently contradictory effects: the duality, for example, of a 'pleasure principle' and a 'death instinct'. One principle is enough for both.

It is hard to imagine that a machine made up of so few parts can cause so much confusion – a machine that is so systematically vexatious and deceptive, because of its simultaneous attraction.

Such is the nature of mimetic desire. It is a stupidly ingenious trap that can cause misfortune under the most diverse circumstances, so much so that it seems beyond human capacities. The semi-clever prefer not to acknowledge it, considering such simplicity an insult to their intelligence (that simplicity, however, is in the service of a certain complexity[2]). They consider it to be nonexistent, illusory, and common knowledge since the foundation of the world.

Those who best understand this form of desire are so disconcerted that they attribute it to the hostile machinations of an evil spirit. Obviously the demon has but one aim: to harm humanity. The Satan of the prologue plays the role that the three friends attribute to God, the same role that the torrent plays in Job's metaphor, the insane community of mimesis.

Desire mistakes its own projections for reality. The image of the torrent describes the world not as it is, but as it appears to men when their desire is exacerbated, when the prohibitions that protect them from implacable rivalries have collapsed.

But the image of the torrent also describes an objective metamorphosis of the world. The initial subjective semblance quickly becomes reality under the influence of desire, which always leaves its mark. Being mimetic, it spreads mimesis everywhere and achieves its own diffusion efficiently, without any effort. We constantly experience the rebound of its ever-increasing effects through the mimetic mirror of the other's desire, so that the world becomes in reality what our desire has made it.

As the world becomes more mimetic it is increasingly more misleading and deceptive, in the same sense as Job's torrent. This is the self-fulfilling prophecy mentioned by Jean-Pierre Dupuy.[3] If I were to believe in a world where the only things worth seeking are not to be found, a world where nothing that is available is worth having, I should share actively in its fabrication. My subjective vision and reality would quickly coalesce, bringing about the disappearance of everything worthy of desire and the creation in ever more monstrous quantities of the undesirable and insignificant.

In a society ruled by mimetic desire, everyone shares in making existence as barren as the desert, but no one is aware of it. As in well-ordered societies, people do only what they see done around them. Paul Dumouchel, Georges-Hubert de Radkowski and the economists of desire have shown this.[4]

Immense regions of the planet have been transformed into deserts by the uses desire-driven men have made of them. The more the desert stretches within us and beyond us, the more we are tempted to blame reality or God himself or, worse still, our neighbour, the first Job who comes along.

In a world controlled by mimetic desire all individuals tend to banish each other, and therefore themselves, to some kind of desert. If we observe this secret relationship between individual situations, the identical alienation in everyone that isolates each one of us, then it is not hard to understand that the appetite for violence may grow and may ultimately be satisfied at that moment when the global tendency to uniformity focuses the mimetic substitutions and polarizations on some victim or other, or perhaps not so randomly but on a victim who is more vulnerable because of his visibility, one who is somehow predestined by the exceptional position he holds in the community – someone like Job.

IV
FROM MECHANISM TO RITUAL

11

The Public Tophet

The role of double mimesis in the history of Job enables us to understand why human communities are driven to follow certain individuals blindly and then to turn against them just as blindly.

Social science has tried to define a typical leader by using such notions as *charisma*. Here we should note the use of the language of the sacred. Charisma comes from *Charis*, meaning grace, who was a goddess. Charisma is defined as if it were yet another characteristic of the leader's personality, like the colour of his hair or the mould of his chin. If that were true the leader's charisma would not be so easily transformed, as it is, into the anti-charisma or counter-charisma of the scapegoat.

Mimetic theory reveals the process by which the mimesis of the obstacle model, the secret source of conflict among homogeneous groups, can result in the mimetic adoption of one single obstacle model, who becomes the scapegoat for absolutely everyone.

The process of choosing a surrogate victim eliminates everyone's antagonism in one move by focusing on a common adversary, and then eliminating the victim. It re-establishes peace, as it were miraculously, and the effect it achieves is magnified by the fact that the suddenly regained unity appears to be the result of the intervention of a supernatural power. This is none other than the scapegoat, who has already been identified in this role by the evil power he is supposed to possess.

This is the origin of the violent sacred, a phenomenon that is much too common in human societies, and too closely implicated in cultural, social, and political events and in the most concrete technical operations, to be dismissed as superstition or collective neurosis, as positivism and psychoanalysis, respectively, have done.

This is a crucial point in the theory. The psychological, moral and social *efficacy* of the scapegoat is identical with its religious function, because its mechanism becomes the perfect source of all social transcendence. The scapegoat phenomena that we observe in our own world reveal only the marginal and rather insignificant aspects of that efficacy.

Because of the relative lack of efficacy in directly observable phenomena, the scapegoat is thought to be incapable of engendering the sacred. The idea that it is capable of major efficacy seems fantastic and unbelievable to most people, yet at the same time they consider it dangerous, scandalous, *not to be mentioned*, as if mention of the idea would promote it and secure the moral approval it lacks in our world.

Silence is never preferable to truth, and in this case the silence has already been broken. We are rather late for this type of revelation. Job was there before us. He defines his own efficacy as scapegoat, which seems much superior to anything we can observe today. He reveals that efficacy in order to weaken the system, not to strengthen it or celebrate its merits; he does not want to provide a moral caution by celebrating its usefulness, nor does he want to recommend it as a form of government.

The persecutors themselves do all this without ever noticing it. Those who have recourse to scapegoats neither mention it nor are aware of it. Those who talk about scapegoats do not make use of them, or if they do, they never make use of those they are talking about:

> I have become a byword among the people,
>   and a creature on whose face to spit.
> My eyes grow dim with grief,
>   and my limbs wear away like a shadow.
> At this honest men are shocked,
>   and the guiltless man rails against the godless;
> just men grow more settled in their ways,
>   those whose hands are clean add strength to strength.
>   (17: 6–9)

The undeserved suffering and downfall of a victim contributes to the good behaviour of his fellow-men; it becomes a principle of moral edification, a miraculous tonic for the social body. The *pharmakos* now becomes the *pharmakon*: the surrogate victim is transformed into a marvellous drug, dangerous but, in moderate doses, capable of curing all illnesses. Had Job been willing to play his role docilely he would undoubtedly soon have been made into a great man, perhaps even a minor divinity.

For everyone to join in the cursing of Job is divine work, since it strengthens the group's harmony and applies a sovereign remedy to the community's wounds. The three friends are doing precisely this. The passage must be seen as a commentary on the behaviour of all 'men of substance'.

We must include among the benefits of the operation the behaviour of the untouchables who ill-treat Job. Thanks to the scapegoat, even the most disinherited participate in a recognized social activity. In fact, thanks to Job, they are partially integrated into the society that excludes them. But it is not just a question of the rabble: at the other extreme of the moral and social ladder *exactly the same thing happens*. The innocent, the righteous, those whose hands are clean – all take great comfort in the misfortune of the scapegoat. Remember Psalm 73.

If our translation is correct, Job is describing in this passage the beneficial effect of his unjust persecution on his own community. I know of no other text where that effect is so bluntly articulated.[1] It is the same as the *tragic effect*, the Aristotelian catharsis, but this is not a theatrical representation, and Job is not trying to embellish the truth of the operation with aesthetic flourishes.

The explicit revelation of the scapegoat mechanism and its consequences is moral in the highest sense of the word, and reveals the imperturbable aestheticism of Aristotle and his literary followers as profoundly immoral.

The translation of this passage is not always the same. As usual, I have chosen the one from the *Jerusalem Bible*, which I recognize as being particularly favourable to my thesis and distinctly different from many others. Ancient and modern translators alike generally make the second part of this text say something vague, which tends to reverse its meaning.

In the *New English Bible* this reversal is carried to the limit, with the following result:

> Honest men are bewildered at this
> and the innocent are indignant at my plight.
> In spite of all, the righteous man maintains his course
> and he whose hands are clean grows strong again.

The man whose hands are clean is doubly strengthened here not *because of*, but *in spite of* the unjust persecution. This interpretation seems to me to be wrong for contextual reasons. What the *New English Bible* would have Job say is contradicted by all the texts we have read. If Job still kept the esteem of the pure and virtuous, he would not be abandoned by absolutely everyone, he would not be the scapegoat which he describes in numerous texts that everyone translates in the same way.

I am not competent to settle the matter linguistically, but I will keep resolutely to the *Jerusalem Bible*. It is the only one in agreement with the context and it is none the less *lectio difficilior* by reason of its paradoxical and subversive character, as well as its opposition to all accepted ideas. I am convinced by arguments pertaining to the global interpretation.

Our translation establishes a direct connection between the persecution of the innocent and the consolation of good citizens, the strengthening of the social order. This connection is so scandalous that many people simply refuse to consider it.

The Book of Job goes so far in its revelation of the scapegoat as the foundation of the sacred, of ethics, of aesthetics and of culture in general that I am not surprised to find such striking formulas as we have just read. If the *Jerusalem Bible* is right, the other translations are evidence of our resistance to such a revelation.

The *Jerusalem Bible* translates the second line of this passage as 'a creature on whose face to spit'. According to Etienne Dhorme,[2] a literal translation would read: 'I will be a public Tophet'. Dhorme indicates in a footnote that, for the commentator Ibn Ezar, the word Tophet is composed of two terms:

> . . . in the first place the valley of the Taphet, a place of shame according to Jeremiah, since it is where the Judaeans practised human sacrifice which was forbidden by Yahveh; they made their sons and daughters go through the fire. Taphet may also mean altar or hearth. The Jews read this word with the vowels of the word *boshet* which means shame.

If we telescope the two terms, combining the vowels of one with the consonants of the second, we get *Tophet*. The *public Tophet*, in this case a man, is an object of unanimous execration. That is to say a *scapegoat*; I see no difference between the two expressions. There is no ambiguity. Despite the numerous tricks language plays on us, I see no reason to complain of its inability to communicate unambiguous meanings.

12

The Orphan Chosen by Lots

The three friends can be numbered among the righteous, who are confirmed in their ways by the sight of the scapegoat. We already know that they are envious. We first saw this envy as it sought satisfaction, in their behaviour towards Job. I will not dwell on that. It is present and explains some things, but not everything. The main interest of the mimesis of envy is that it sets the scapegoat mechanism in motion. The Job whom the friends pursue is no longer merely an envied rival, but a scapegoat for the whole community.

Are the two the same? They are, but only because of the scapegoat mechanism. Thanks to that mechanism, personal resentment re-enforces rather than opposes the social bond. Instead of fostering discord, it brings about concord. Any opposition between the individual and the group disappears. In the strange but banal social communion that Job describes, the sinister envy of the friends is transcended without being repressed or sublimated, in the Freudian sense. This is precisely the incomparable value of the scapegoat mechanism for society.

My interpretation is neither psychological nor sociological. Nor is it religious in the humanist tradition. The discovery of the scapegoat mechanism blurs the traditional divisions between disciplines.

The scapegoat mechanism determines the religious dimension of what happens in the Dialogues, except for a few extraordinary passages to be discussed in my conclusion. The sense of religion to which the friends and their society cling is not a vague general idea that distantly controls an affair that ultimately they themselves can regard as purely human.

Religion, for them, is all that can and cannot be observed of the scapegoat mechanism: its immediate and ultimate effects, the actions it sets in motion, the circumstances which foster it and which discourage it.

Like a bolt of lightning, the scapegoat mechanism suddenly frees all men without being answerable to anyone except perhaps to the victim himself, who is likely to become an idol after his disappearance. No one can control or manipulate the mechanism. It bears all the marks of a supernatural intervention. Everything about it suggests a power that transcends wretched humanity. It is the prototype of every sacred epiphany.

It is not difficult to imagine that religious men might devote body and soul to this mystery that saves them. There is no difference, in this respect as in any other, between the three friends and those who surround them. Society is very aware that it has a good thing in its victim, a successful purge for ill feelings. It is equally aware that the process is as dangerous as it is beneficial. It is activated only at the end of a period of uncertainty and disturbance, a period marked by a disorder and violence that are in danger of accelerating.

The community, therefore, needs self-confident men who will endeavour not to stifle violence at birth, as in our day, but to prevent it from spreading randomly within the community, steering it towards the best victim, one who is most likely to attract unanimous opposition. This victim may be singled out beforehand in the eyes of the envious and the malcontent by exceptional success and extraordinary responsibilities, and is thus already a victim targeted for divine anger.

Beneath the attitude of the friends, especially Eliphaz, we sense their willingness to go along with the phenomenon and imitate all the actions which have previously led to its successful outcome. Its most desirable orientation must be maintained and this would appear, from all the evidence, to be its present one. This is the primary purpose of the passionate speeches about the celestial armies.

What I am describing is ritual inspiration. It flows logically from the scapegoat mechanism. Persecutors do not know why this mechanism has such a beneficial effect on their mutual relationships and the entire community, but they are aware of its operation and are very receptive to it. Its every indication is received favourably. Everything possible is done to encourage its repetition, which is why Job cannot count on any of his former 'friends'.

Once more, the friends are not there to 'comfort' Job, as the prologue has the gall to proclaim, nor are they there simply to enjoy his discomfiture. They are important men who do not put themselves out without good reason. Not only – as I have explained – do they represent the community, but they are fulfilling a social and religious function. They are there to watch over the successful operation of the scapegoat mechanism.

Like Greek choruses, the rhythmic clamour of the three series of speeches reminds us of ritual recitations intended to excite participants to a religious fury. The repetitive quality of these incantations mimics the movement and shouts of a crowd as it begins to polarize itself in opposition to a victim.

What is sought is a mimetic effect on the whole gathering of people. Since there was already a tendency for the violence to focus on Job, it must be used to its fullest. Once the victim is designated, he no longer counts as an individual. His only value is to serve to polarize any errant violence in the community. By converging together on the one object, all sources of division, all forces that tear each other apart under many different pretexts, are transformed into factors of unity. Without that convergence, the worst could happen.

The three persons appear to be very exalted, but they never deviate from an extremely classical scenario. There is method in their trance. From all indications they are not improvising, and their finest flights are proven formulas and fairly venerable religious imprecations.

The friends' speeches give off a waft of primitive liturgy that prompts our recognition of a kind of ritual in this process. It could be called 'the ritual of the *ancient trail*', the ritual of Eliphaz.

Former instances of similar events inevitably serve as models. For a happy conclusion to be reached, the community must appeal to the forefathers, men known for their experience and wisdom. They have survived similar storms unharmed. What is happening to Job did not happen to them. Eliphaz, particularly, reminds us of a priest. He is always the first to speak; he obviously enjoys great authority. It is he who announces the probable repetition of 'divine vengeance'.

If, in the story of Job, the characteristics I have enumerated are truly present, then it can be seen as a sort of sacrifice, or perhaps what anthropologists like Frazer call a *scapegoat rite*. In both cases repetition of the scapegoat mechanism must be ensured, either by sacrificing a victim or by expelling him violently from the community.

Under the direction of Eliphaz, and before our very eyes, the three give themselves over to what specialists in ritual call a *sacrificial preparation*. It consists of stirring up the participants, usually the entire community, to the point of effervescence, at which time the necessary violence will be so spontaneous that it will seem that the mechanism has been set in motion of its own accord. The final immolation must be made to look as much as possible like the natural orgasm of collective violence, the final paroxysm of a mob soon to be incited. In order to prevent this compressed violence from spreading dangerously and being unleashed elsewhere than on the victim, ritual vigilance surrounds the process with all sorts of precautions.

If this is the case, and if Job is as skilful at revealing the true meaning of his ordeal as the community is at hiding it, we can expect him to make some scathing allusions to the sacrificial cuisine of which he is the main course. And we are not mistaken. Here is the sort of reproach he makes to the three 'friends':

Soon you will be casting lots for an orphan,
    and selling your friend at bargain prices! (6: 27)

In societies where human sacrifice is practised, orphans are the chosen victims. The sacrifice of a child whose parents are living runs the risk of making enemies of them.

The procedures for selecting victims bear the stamp of sly caution aimed at preventing the spread of any violence by eliminating any potential ambiguities, any uncertainties that might lead to dispute. The temptation for the community to become the victim's champions is reduced to the minimum by sacrificing an orphan, with the result that there is very little risk of adding oil to the flames of violence. The chances of the sacrifice being effective are maximized.

A sinister 'sacrificial wisdom' dictates the choice of orphans to those offering the sacrifice, and inspires the idea of lottery. If the choice of the victim is left to the calculation of the sacrificers, there is always risk of discord. It must therefore be left to chance, a pattern that is familiar to those who sacrifice in spontaneous gatherings, thereby constituting the real phenomenon of the scapegoat, and the ideal model of the perfectly achieved sacrifice.

The orphan chosen by lottery is a *ritual* scapegoat, a substitute for that original victim who spontaneously united everyone in opposition to himself and reconciled the community by his death. To re-establish unity, a unanimous agreement without any second thoughts is needed.

Job implicitly compares himself with the ideal victim, the being who has no relatives, servants, neighbours, nor even a friend to defend him. He can be chosen without fear of reviving the divisions that the sacrifice is meant to heal. Job rephrases in sacrificial terms all that we have understood in realistic style. He is abandoned by everyone; the void surrounds him. His alleged friends aggravate the situation by suggesting that he could be recognized as the latest of the 'wicked', the 'perverse', the 'enemies of God'.

Job's tone is gloomily ironic. For his words to carry their full weight, they need to be understood within the context of a world in which human sacrifice properly speaking has been officially abolished, already discredited by a higher religion, but not so completely forgotten that an allusion to an orphan chosen by lots is not still understood. Perhaps child sacrifice is still being practised in secret in some retrograde circles.

In Job's eyes, the three friends are trafficking in human flesh. They seem honourable and they are honourable from their own perspective, that of their religious system, but in the universe Job has entered they remind us of somewhat shady experts who have the necessary skill and knowledge to carry out the most sordid affairs without attracting any attention.

Everything seems clear in the case of Job. Is it not merely an honest debate over the question of Evil and the reality of divine providence? There should not be any improper details: but there are and, mysteriously, they are always arranged by those people who appear so reliable and worthy of confidence, clearly marked for this sort of undertaking – no doubt because in reality they are not in the least bit reliable and worthy of confidence.

The friends regard the sacrifice of Job as socially therapeutic. It is not so much a question of curing certain individuals as of watching over the well-being of the entire community. This is reminiscent of the shamans, of all the *medicine men* who operate by purifications and eliminations. Here, too, there is always an 'ancient trail' to serve as model and the same itinerary is always rediscovered.

Like shamans, our friends have their supernatural visions; they evoke great battles which take place in the heavens, but they never lose sight of what is happening on the earth. Like vultures squatting near a future carcass, they watch over his agony. They fulfil the sanitary function of the vultures in certain traditional civilizations. In *Oedipus Rex*, one of the perspectives on the expulsion of the scapegoat is essentially 'medical' or 'hygienic'.

Here is another of Job's observations, which summarizes these last remarks – another awesome observation addressed to the three 'friends':

   As for you, you are only charlatans,
      physicians in your own estimation. (13: 4)

Philippe Nemo[1] has the excellent idea of annexing the friends'
religion to the domain of technique. I will add only that it is a
question of the oldest of all techniques, the mother of them all:
the technique of the scapegoat.

13

Origin and Repetition

If the crowd phenomena, for which Job is the pretext rather than the cause, constitute a ritual, then they cannot be a part of the actual scapegoat mechanism itself, or of the spontaneous collective violence, or of the original lynching. So far I have implied that what is revealed in the Dialogues is not just another ritual but the model for them all, the origin that was postulated in *Violence and the Sacred*. Is that an illusion which must be renounced?

In a certain sense, yes. Strictly speaking, the ritual dimension is indispensable to the theory. The mechanism in its pure state could appear only under an exclusively mythological form, at least for Eliphaz and his companions, which is not exactly true of the discourses of the ancient trail. Job's case must be considered separately. From the persecutors' perspective, the sociological aspect of the phenomenon should not show through as it does in several places.

Once recognized, the mechanism is no longer completely spontaneous. Its repetition receives support and assistance, hardly distinguishable from the early stages of ritualization. In other words, no matter how incomplete it is, the recognition of the mechanism has the effect of gradually transforming its operation. Rituals are merely the first stages of this transformation.

There are still other reasons why the process as represented cannot be 'original'. It does not initiate the creation of new gods, but rather is inscribed in a ready-made religious framework. Inevitably it blends with ritual practice. Thus its ritual character must be identified and then immediately attenuated. If we once more examine Eliphaz's main question to Job: 'And will you still follow the ancient trail trodden by the wicked?', we will easily sense that it belongs at the heart of a ritual.

Certainly Job is not the one to decide whether he will tread the ancient trail. He has set out on it against his will. Yet Eliphaz is perfectly sincere and is not mocking him. Job makes no decision, but neither does Eliphaz. No one decides, no one can really control the mechanism. There are certainly plots against Job, but they are not part of a sacrificial plan. The crowd always seems to be responsible for unleashing the fatal process. As long as the affair is not completely premeditated and controlled in advance, then there is no true ritualization. A true rite would depend exclusively on those who are charged with its execution. We are not at that point.

Eliphaz's question is not pure rhetoric. In this character's mind there is some uncertainty, and because he is a persecutor he turns to the victim to dispel it, not to the crowd to which he belongs. Like everyone else, he is deceived by the scapegoat mechanism which he, however, helps to activate.

The idea that the answer rests with Job, that the scapegoat can change his direction, choose the trail of his liking – in other words that he is an actor rather than a puppet – is again a typical concept of a persecutor, the generative illusion of the scapegoat mechanism.

Job has nothing really to do with the priests who choose some victim by lot, from a kind of pool which is made up of all those who satisfy certain general conditions of admissibility. He has nothing to do with shamans who autocratically decide on rites of exorcism. His metaphors are genuine when he stigmatizes the role of the friends, but they should not be taken literally. They are polemical. They provide a part, but only a part, of the rhetoric.

This is not an example of the language of persecutors who place all responsibility on the victims, but of a completely new rhetoric of the persecuted that does the reverse. It tends to exaggerate the responsibility, nevertheless real, of every persecutor.

The role of the friends is more limited. They cannot choose whom they will send along the ancient trail, nor at what moment. They have no control over either travellers or journeys. They are there merely to control the traffic.

Job's affair need not have taken place when it did, or even at all. Job's savage resistance perhaps prevents it from coming to a climax and, retrospectively, justifies the uncertainty that motivates Eliphaz's question, but that uncertainty was already present; it was not born out of Job's heroic behaviour. It can be found in the narrator of Psalm 73.

Thus the schema of the ancient trail is somewhat ambiguous. It is not purely accidental, but it is too dependent on the unforeseen behaviour of the crowd to be clearly ritual. It is between the two: too similar to a riot to be defined in ritual terms, too ritualized to be recognized as the raw form of the scapegoat mechanism.

We are not at the dawn of a new sacrificial culture, but rather at the mid-point of decline of the old, at the moment of sacrificial crisis. But at the heart of this fatal crisis are certain occurrences that resemble beginnings. The crowd phenomena as portrayed have retained or rediscovered a virulence that makes them very similar to the original scapegoat mechanism.

These phenomena provide an excellent image of the original mechanism, coming after its origin but before its rituals have become truly specific and well differentiated. Without being the origin, they are close enough in time to resemble it more closely than any form of rite.

I have compared Job's situation to a carnival. But it can no more be compared with a real festival, however primitive, than Job with the victim of a genuine sacrifice. I hold to my comparison but that is all it is, a comparison.

Job himself probably compares his friends to ritual doctors. All these comparisons shed light on some aspects of what is happening, but they conceal or distort others. The Job affair resembles many kinds of rites but is not truly comparable to any of them. How can that be?

For my answer, I will again refer to the mimetic-scapegoat

thesis which reappears at every stage of my work. The original scapegoat is imitated in religious ceremonies by those who have spontaneously benefited from him, and then by their descendants, and so becomes the origin of all rituals.

The reason the story of Job resembles so many rituals without ever being equivalent to them is that it is more spontaneous than any rite. It is close enough to the original violence to herald and prefigure the determined forms that it did not engender, and that it will not engender, although it could theoretically do so at the end of a more advanced ritualization.

If the story of Job provides an adequate representation of the origin it can be used to replace it, hypothetically, in order to show that prolonged imitation and more advanced ritualization would easily achieve a metamorphosis of all the ritual forms mentioned, including the most remarkable, which I have not yet described.

In order to 'reduce' all rites to a common origin it would seem necessary to ignore the considerable differences that separate them. But it is Job himself who suggests that we must compare apparently irreducible elements when he likens himself, in turn, to two ritual figures that it would seem absurd to compare. We already know the first, the orphan who has been sacrificed. The second is . . . the sacred king.

This is also familiar. We cannot forget Job's emotional recollection of his former successes with the people, before he became a scapegoat. The people's veneration had made him a master who was always obeyed. Let us look at the last three lines of the passage already quoted:

> In a lordly style, I told them which course to take,
> and like a king amid his armies,
> I led them where I chose. (29: 25)

Everything else is in keeping; before his fall, Job truly enjoyed a power and a prestige comparable to that of a sacred king, a truly living god.

This kingly connection, far from ending with Job's metamorphosis into a persecuted victim, becomes spectacularly fulfilled. The final Job is hardly royal in our eyes, but that is true only for us. Monarchy signifies for us a modern monarchy, desacralized, apparently unrelated to sacrifice except in periods of revolution. We do not perceive that in the ancient and primitive sense of sacred royalty, the scapegoat is more royal than ever. The persecution phase does not destroy the resemblance; it perfects it.

During the normal exercise of his prerogatives the king, like Job before his disaster, lives on a higher level than common humanity, but at certain critical moments his position is reversed. He is humiliated, challenged, brutalized and often even assassinated.

The overthrow of the king is characteristically a ritual practice that varies enormously from one monarchy to another, but the one common denominator is that the monarch plays the role of victim, either symbolic or more or less real. During these rites the subjects pretend to forget their idolatory, while they briefly revolt against their idol. Veneration is transformed into execration. Certain African rites clearly attribute a primary role to this turnabout on the part of the people. As in the case of Job, the monarchy is characterized by the very intense and double nature of the relationships between a single individual on the one hand and an entire group on the other.

14

Job and the Sacred King

Of all the complex ritual forms, monarchy provides the most remarkable analogies with the career of Job or of Oedipus. I am not the first to whom this has occurred.

Does this mean, as has been said,[1] that royal rites had a direct and external influence on the conception of the Dialogues? Was the author thinking of real monarchy, and did this inspire his portrayal of Job's fortunes and misfortunes, the double career of the protagonist?

If Job were modelled on a royal rite, the insults he is made to endure would have a ritual character. We would expect to recognize in them a hieratic and solemn element that is hardly in keeping with the devastated amazement of the scapegoat, and with all that is 'existential' in the texts we have read. Instead of being surprised by the indignities inflicted on him, someone participating in a rite would know what to expect too well to speak about it with such emotion. Job's passion does not resemble a ritual experience. The story of Job cannot feasibly be modelled on a rite.

There is another reason for doubting that Job is patterned on a specific rite: his experience resembles not one rite, but many. His symbolic radiance is the same as that of Greek tragedy, but greater. If Job were inspired by a real monarchy, then all the more reason for *Oedipus Rex* to be. The creative genius of Sophocles certainly cannot be imprisoned in the narrowness of a rite.

The ritual thesis is more interesting than the moral commentaries. It draws attention to the vast areas of the Dialogues where no one ventures, but it is inaccurate. It misconstrues everything. It starts with a rite in order to understand the

Dialogues, when it should really begin in the reverse direction. One must begin with the crowd phenomena described in Job in order to understand rituals. What Job is describing should be recognized as the original mould of all rituals. The proximity of that origin endows the Dialogues with their extraordinary symbolic radiance.

If the mimetic-scapegoat thesis is correct, to end up with sacred monarchy it is enough simply to prolong and strengthen the process of imitation/ritualization evolving around Job.

Even when repetitions of the scapegoat mechanism remain spontaneous, they tend to slip into the mould of prior phenomena. It is their natural course when encouraged and flattered, as we have seen, by the behaviour of the friends. It is easy to understand that repetition will cause the mechanism to lose its spontaneity so that, ultimately, it will no longer be a mechanism but become transformed into a series of deliberate actions, words and ritual prescriptions. This metamorphosis is all the more likely because as the repetition becomes more rhythmic and regular, it tends to eliminate any unforeseen and brutal variations that may spontaneously set the phenomenon in motion. As the rite calms the community, it loses its earlier virulence and acquires the connotations generally contained in the term 'ritual'.

There must come a time when nothing else is left to chance. When the duly appointed 'wicked man' has reached the end of his journey, and has been appropriately lynched, then an official successor is appointed. Efficiency requires an immediate appointment. Delays, which might hurt the community, are avoided. There is only one way to ensure that a sufficiently wicked person is appointed: he must be made to commit all the crimes attributed to his predecessors.

A phase of frenzied idolatry follows immediately. The victim is expected to exert limitless power over the community, as demanded by the original model. Remember the nostalgic recollections of Job in Chapter 29: the future victim reigns over his future executioners for the same amount of time as his predecessors, precisely to the day, which is also rigidly determined by previous examples; then, in a single movement, the people turn on their idol to persecute and sacrifice him.

If we accept that the story of Job serves as *model*, we are able to see the whole of the ritual system of monarchy from one end to the other. There is no doubt that the imaginary 'crimes' of the scapegoat can be identified in sacred monarchy. In most cases, the system offers a quite significant combination of the crimes attributed to both Job and Oedipus. The king is criticized for his arrogance, brutality and even ferocity. He is that same oppressor of the people as the 'wicked men' described by Eliphaz. For good measure, the king is expected to confess officially to a certain number of oedipal crimes: the murder of a father or a close relative, or some well-concocted incestuous relationship with a mother or sister.

What could be simpler in creating another public Tophet than to demand that he actually carry out the infamous actions attributed to his predecessors? These crimes often take place just before what they are supposed to set in motion: the transformation of the monarch into a scapegoat. This is often also the beginning of the ritual sequence. The king must demonstrate his ability to carry out the major social function of a 'wicked man'. It is the *sine qua non* for accession to what is about to become the royal throne.

The actions required of the king, in monarchic rites, are the same as those for which Job or Oedipus is reproached, but their meaning is often different. This difference does not constitute a valid objection to the thesis of their common origin. Far from it. The change in meaning is part of the process of ritualization. The crimes are scarcely crimes any longer, or are not crimes at all but rather initiation rites into the ambiguous power of the king; sometimes they may even be regarded as heroic deeds.

Requiring the supposed criminal to commit a certain crime always has long-term consequences. A forbidden action that is turned into a basic duty does not remain a crime for long. The forbidden and the obligatory are opposites that cannot fail to react on each other when combined.

The obligatory inevitably prevails over the forbidden, since there is only one concern in ritual: efficacy, the upholding of public order and the prevention of uncontrollable chaos. The fact that the scapegoat's 'crimes' tend to become initiation tests or even, ultimately, acts of bravado does not permit us to doubt the initially criminal character of the required deeds.

If either the obligation is forbidden or the forbidden becomes obligatory, then both meanings are overturned and a third emerges that seems entirely new but is really a combination of the other two. It takes very little reflection to understand that the new meaning is indeed the same as the one in real monarchies, that of an initiation test. Royalty is so extraordinary that it demands very special rites. The former criminal connotation is still perceptible behind the popular idea of the king as an exceptionally daring fellow. He proves this by undertakings which would be considered crimes among common people.

The more scrupulous the imitation, the more the forbidden acts required of the king become strict duties and therefore cease to be crimes, but only for the monarch.

The former crimes of the scapegoat have become coronation rites. Thus ritual imitation gives birth to significant forms. Paradoxically, the more conservative it wishes to be, the more creative it becomes. The more accurate and strict it tries to be, the more it transforms the scapegoat's 'crimes' and the faster it empties them of their original meaning.

Only if everyone is convinced of the culprit's true guilt can the rite be efficacious. The king must become the criminal the scapegoat has always been. Here we have a proof that the persecutors and their descendants are not cynically manipulating the scapegoating process; on the contrary, instead of manipulating it they are trying their hardest to re-create absolutely all the circumstances which they hope will again release the saving mechanism, *because in the past that is what they have done.*

The crimes are real crimes in the beginning, and evidence of the criminal connotation is too frequent to allow any doubt about the reality of this belief. The schema of the tyrannical king who is oppressive and incestuous and is finally sacrificed, either in reality or symbolically, is only an 'ancient trail' so well marked that it is unrecognizable. From now on, the journey is rigidly determined.

The scapegoat mechanism was pure spontaneity. From the point at which it is programmed from beginning to end, it ceases inevitably to be itself. Ritual imitation is the exact opposite of spontaneity. The greater its triumph, the more the ritual becomes the purely mechanical, sterile and dead activity we call rite.

15

The Evolution of Ritual

We should resuscitate the idea that rituals evolve, stressing the fact that they evolve because they are rigidly imitative of a more and more distorted representation of the original scapegoating. We must ask, however, why ritual imitation gives rise to such different forms as the king and the orphan chosen by lots.

Royalty can obviously be distinguished by the absolute power of the king. The model for this power is found in the first phase of crowd phenomena described in Job, during which the future victim is the idol of his future executioners.

Sacred monarchy is characterized by the predominance of the first phase over the second: this is why we speak of royalty. In any institution in which the chief person is not first and foremost a living idol, an omnipotent master, rather than a scapegoat we recognize something other than a monarchy, including a sacred monarchy.

This predominance of the first phase is a general prerequisite of monarchy; but the minute we examine real monarchies, we are aware of varying degrees. The second phase is toned down, reduced, or worn away in proportion to the predominance of the first phase. The two phases are always out of balance, either very slightly or to such a degree that the scapegoat phase totally disappears.

In some monarchies, even in recent times, the king was actually sacrificed. There is no reason to doubt this fact on the pretext that in other monarchies the sacrifice was more apparent than real: in this case, either another victim was sacrificed in place of the king or there was only a pretence of sacrificing the king.

In Babylon and elsewhere, something else took place that is singularly reminiscent of Job's experience. Once a year the king was humiliated, insulted and abused by the crowd – even beaten. There seemed to be no question of killing him, even symbolically. In still other monarchies, all real violence is excluded. There is not even a pretence of persecuting or killing the king, but vestiges of the symbolism of victims frequently remain. Finally there are existing monarchies free of the symbolism of victims. The monarch's sovereignty is never interrupted or challenged, even by a faint memory of the scapegoating process. This is the monarchy of modern times. (Admittedly, real revolutions occur that replace the old rituals. Thus we have a return of the generative mechanism, a return which is inevitably fruitless in our world.)

If we look at the global situation, the entire panorama of ritual, we see – not only in monarchies, but everywhere – that things automatically organize themselves according to the principle I have described: two phases out of equilibrium. They appear to be struggling for complete possession of the territory of ritual. As one of the two prevails, the ritual phenomena begin to resemble more and more the well-differentiated institutions which we imagined in the first place, but which must be the ultimate result of a double process of morphogenisis.

The greater the distance between the monarchy and the model it imitates, the more of a monarchy and less of a sacrifice it becomes. It is increasingly difficult to apprehend its origin in the scapegoat mechanism, which naturally encourages the belief that it never was and never could be founded on such a mechanism. Any survival of sacrificial traits must be interpreted as the hypocritical theatrics of a power hiding its tyrannical nature. But monarchy hides nothing at all.

In any case, there is nothing theatrical about the continuity of intermediary forms, the existence of an almost complete series of stages between on the one hand, the royal rituals that are loosely linked to victims and resemble popular uprisings and on the other, the rites that have been cleansed of every symbolic violence. This continuity suggests a slow evolution towards the modern desacralized monarchy, beginning with a double crowd phenomenon like the one portrayed in the text of Job.

What I am suggesting is not really a classification, in the sense that the stages are only stages. They do not correspond to any institution that can be defined, nor can they be organized into structural oppositions. They suggest an evolutionary dynamism that begins with Job as a religiously imitated model with both its phases emphasized, and gradually moves without any precise transition in the direction of what we term modern monarchy – that is, a pure power that has been desacralized, relieved of all that recalls its 'opposite', the scapegoat. Because of our bias against history we look on this power as a sort of innate idea, a pure chemical element, a point of departure. It is more likely the outcome not of a single, but of many evolutions.

In short, the rituals I have been describing emphasize the first phase of idolatrous relationship between the people and the man who, for that reason, becomes king. This preference becomes increasingly exaggerated to the detriment of the alternate phase of the scapegoat, who becomes a symbolic show and finally disappears altogether.

Why this tendency? Is it a monarchy cleansed of ritual, or some desire for power in its pure state, that retrospectively directs the evolution? Is there really an innate idea, or a Platonic being that serves as an 'attractor'? Is the evolution predetermined by the form in which it results? It is none of these, as we shall see when we learn that in addition to the monarchies I have defined, which come into being by virtue of this particular imbalance, other systems exist that come into being because of that same imbalance, but the other way round.

This time, the scapegoat phase predominates to the detriment of the popular idol, who tends to disappear; yet enough vestiges of the latter remain to ensure that he is given as serious consideration as the vestiges of the second phase are in the case of sacred monarchies.

Let us take, for example, the sacrifice of orphans or the immolation of young defenceless virgins in the ancient world – in early Greece, in the Mesoamerican cultures, and other places. These ritual forms frequently present a first phase, more or less long, during which the future victim enjoys almost royal privelges: all his orders are obeyed and all his wishes fulfilled.

This sort of behaviour has never really been understood. Only a belated explanation is provided. When ethnologists speak of it, they always revert to the idea of a kind of 'compensation' accorded to the victim by the persecutors. At bottom the sacrificers are good souls who take pity on the innocents they are about to exterminate; they do everything in their power to make their last moments enjoyable. These explanations merely draw attention to what they are trying to hide – the fact that those who carry out the sacrifice are persecutors.

We must recognize in these phenomena that appear bizarre in the context of a sacrifice – as bizarre as the persecution or even symbolic immolation of the king in the context of monarchy – the vestiges of the first, popular idol phase. The umbilical cord which is a link with the crowd phenomena observed in Job has not been completely broken. It is the same evolution as in sacred royalty, but completely reversed. Here again we find a whole range of intermediary forms, from a slight imbalance to the complete disappearance of the phase, which tends to atrophy.

Yet this phase survives in too many of the sacrificial rituals scattered across the entire planet for us to ignore it without further examination, or to pretend that every variation is a uniquely independent cultural form. The thesis of the 'infinite creativity' of human cultures is inspired by the most mediocre romanticism. So long as the 'aberrant' vestiges in rites and institutions are not put on the same level as the facts we consider 'normal' and appropriate, human culture will never be understood. But are we really trying to understand it?

What is the explanation for the two symmetrical series of ritual and post-ritual phenomena, characterized by a growing imbalance between the two phases of the model imitated? Is the course of evolution secretly controlled not by one but, in this case, by two pre-existent forms, the 'true' monarchy on the one hand and the 'true' sacrifice on the other?

Obviously, 'true' monarchy and sacrifice exist only in minds distorted by Platonic essentialism and its modern substitutes, the Cartesianism of clear and distinct ideas, of which the latest variant is structuralism. We should do without this essentialism, even in its linguistic form. Our two series of symmetrical imbalances are more easily interpreted without it.

Like the deritualized king, the sacrificed orphan is the result of an increasingly one-sided ritual imitation. In the first case, the idol phase triumphs and causes the disappearance of the scapegoat aspects. In the second, it is the reverse: the scapegoat wins out and the idol gradually disappears.

Clearly it is not a deep-rooted preference for one or the other phase, nor their content, that determines the tendency of rituals to favour one or the other, since evolution can take place equally in either direction. What, then, is the source of this tendency? If there is no question of a positive force, a permanent inclination for one direction or the other, then it must be an aversion to maintaining the two phases together, an antipathy towards the *conjunction* of these two phases.

The system is not extremely complex but must appear so to ritual imitation, which attempts to impoverish or simplify it. I do not think this is a conscious aim of ritual. It tries to preserve the model it is imitating in its entirety, but never succeeds. The model juxtaposes details that appear more and more contradictory the greater the distance from the origin – beginning, of course, with the idol and the scapegoat.

In order to emphasize simultaneously the two phases of the model, everything must be interpreted in terms of mimesis, as I have done; ritual thought neither wants to nor can do this: mimesis which does not differentiate is fundamentally inimical to the ritual inspiration.

The permanent tendency of religious thought causes rites to evolve always and everywhere. The place occupied by a ritual on either of the two scales reveals the system's degree of evolution in relation to its own diachrony. Global evolution always moves in the same direction, and the possibility of a universal history is not excluded.

Just as there exists a logic of envious imitation, so there also exists a logic of religious imitation and we have only to develop it – beginning with the 'ancient trail' of Eliphaz – and discover its incompatibilities and the productive tensions it creates, to understand why it becomes a force for the creation of forms. From a single point of departure, it gives birth to the most diverse institutions. A dynamic of ritual imitation preserves certain things from the origin but others, inevitably, are modified and even lost.

Whereas the logic of mimetic desire destroys the differences it seeks, that of religious imitation creates differences it does not seek. It aspires only to the faithful reproduction of the model.

Whatever the role mimetic desire plays in our 'passions' and in our behaviour, our intellect prefers to ignore its presence and seek recourse in the alterntative logic. To understand this we need only observe modern criticism of great texts, for the process of mimetic scapegoating remains unseen even in those great works that make it most explicit.

The commentaries on the Book of Job provide the best example of this. On reading the texts, some will grant that Job is a scapegoat and are forced to acknowledge that the theme is present in the work. They will also acknowledge the theme of the popular idol.

But they will resist the conjunction of these two phases, especially in its mimetic interpretation which asserts the crucial role of this conjunction without making it a causal conjunction in the ordinary sense. They will not accept it even though our own world provides examples of it. The tyranny of fashion, political, cultural and professional life, the sexual parades, constantly reproduce combinations of idolatry and ostracism that – though less violent – are identical in structure with what we learn about in the words of Job.

Ritual imitation differentiates, distinguishes, simplifies, organizes and classifies data in such a way as always to mutilate, destroy and hide mimetic mechanisms, especially that of the scapegoat, whose differentiating and mystifying effects it endlessly prolongs. Ritual thought can never fully grasp its own origin, which is perpetuated in philosophical thought and, today, in the social sciences that have inherited the powers of rite as well as its basic impotence.

Ritual cannot seem to focus on a single aspect of the original model without neglecting all other aspects, which then dwindle and disappear. Ritual imitation acquires its creative force through an unconscious process of mutilation and transformation that results in an extreme variety of religious and non-religious institutions.

Even in the early stages of the process, when the two phases are almost intact, the process cannot be in perfect balance. However lightly, the system always leans in one direction or the other. As it develops, the original divergence will determine the entire evolution.

Two slopes appear. Once the ritual imitators unwittingly embark in one direction, they continue in that chosen direction because they are influenced by the principles that control their imitation. Ultimately, the process will result in forms that have been so metamorphosed that they will seem completely different, and sufficiently simplified to appear 'elementary' and 'fundamental', predating the bizarre complexity of the model proposed by Job.

We therefore have victims who are only victims and kings who are none other than kings. And philosophical idealism, which is ineradicable, does the rest. Everything must be the opposite of what I describe, since well-differentiated concepts come at the end. Thus if we have absolutely no understanding of what sacrifice is, the institution seems 'simple' enough to constitute a good 'idea', in the Platonic sense, whereas Job's predicament is a kind of monster.

Ethnologists today are impatient when we insist that something of the idol remains in the victim of a sacrifice, or that there is something of the victim in the all-powerful monarch. In their view, such concepts as 'monarchy' and 'sacrifice' came first and have no history. All genetic hypotheses are ruled out.

From Aristotle to structuralism, all ideas of static classification are the late products of a ritual mentality. The recent insistence on a differential linguistics is merely another recipe for the perpetuation of this immense tradition, behind which there is always essentialism, the fundamental Platonism of a philosophy which, throughout history, remains true to the great trends of ritual inspiration.

Fortunately, the extreme conservatism of ritual always leaves traces which enable us to recover the truth. The vast majority of rites retain enough symmetrical traces of the phase that is on its way out to make my thesis the only plausible one. Faintly visible behind the most dissimilar rituals is a double relationship with the crowd, similar to that which makes Job alternately both idol and scapegoat for the same people.

The fact that even the most transformed rituals preserve traces of the atrophied phase is in keeping with what we find at the other end of the scale, rituals that have developed so little and are so close to the original model that the two phases are clearly discernible. They carry approximately the same weight, and the original model of the idol/scapegoat is completely recognizable.

These are rituals that still hesitate between the two slopes. We find in them the crowd phenomena described in Job, but in such violent form that our attention is deflected from their essence and the 'classicism' of their form escapes us.

These rituals retain the integrity of the two phases, emphasizing each in turn. This produces forms that appear to be extremely confusing, but not to a mimetic interpretation, since they have exactly the same profile as the double experience of Job.

Such would seem to be the case of the cannibalism of the north-east of Brazil, as described by the first explorers.

Although they were about to be sacrificed at the cannibalistic feast, the prisoners of ritual wars were treated with great respect by their captors. They were given women; they enjoyed certain privileges. Sometimes this situation lasted for years, until the prescribed day when they would be devoutly massacred and devoured. This is the same perfectly programmed schema as the ancient trail, with the addition of cannibalism, which changes nothing essential.

An apparently minor custom that is nevertheless always mentioned is for me the most revealing. Just before the crucial moment of the great cannibalistic orgy which is the local variation of the scapegoat scene, the future victim is encouraged to escape, something that is normally forbidden, or to commit some other transgression that would make him guilty in the eyes of the community – that would make him, in other words, someone capable of uniting this same crowd in opposition to himself. Before the victim is killed, he is insulted and abused with a gratuitous ferocity that recalls precisely what Job describes.

Although it is unquestionably ritual, the system retains a large dose of spontaneity. It cannot truly be described in terms of monarchy, nor in terms of sacrifice. Yet it partakes of both institutions. This cannibalism goes back to the point in time when the ancient trail is either about to be transformed into a rite or else, for some reason or other, is halted in its development.

The real difference in comparison with the ancient trail is found in the ritual principle itself. Those who practice those rites know at the outset that their idol is not destined always to remain an idol, since deliberate preparations for the dramatic conclusion are in progress. But this knowledge has little influence on the attitude towards the future victim during the 'idolatrous' phase.

The infraction the prisoner is invited to commit helps to mobilize the crowd against him. The rite prescribes exactly what is required to arouse hostility towards the victim at the precise instant demanded by the operation of the scapegoat mechanism. We should not conclude, in this case either, that those who practise the ritual are cynically manipulating a scapegoat mechanism whose operation is known to them. We should not imagine that behind this ritual prescription there exists a knowledge of the type exemplified by Job and other great biblical figures. It is exactly the opposite. The Indians believe they are massacring someone who is really guilty, because of their blind belief in the real guilt of those whom they have massacred before.

It is almost impossible to imagine the 'friends' forcing Job to commit the crimes of which they accuse him in order to make sure, finally, that he really has committed them and to give back to the community another 'wicked man', duly authenticated. It is not cynicism on their part; rather their professional conscience.

Our South-American cannibalistic rites contradict the prevailing neo-Rousseauism too much for the claim not to arise that the early ethnographic descriptions of them must be fictitious: I think, however, that, as a rule they are accurate. We have absolutely no reason to doubt the reality of the system described by sixteenth-century observers.

Their truthfulness is guaranteed by the perfectly clear picture they give of the intention that motivates the cannibalistic practices. If a European observer had perceived in these rites a desire to repeat the type of scapegoat mechanism described by Job, we could suppose that he might have invented some of the most striking resemblances to make his point. But there is no such desire, and yet the details are still there.

Thus it is inconceivable that these details were invented rather than really belonging to the ritual practice described. The situation is somewhat similar to a messenger being charged to transcribe a message, letter by letter, in a language he does not know. If the transmitted message is linguistically correct and perfectly comprehensible, we can be certain that it has been faithfully copied. The messenger has added nothing of his own. If he had changed something, being ignorant of the language, he could easily have made it *incoherent*. He would not have been capable of making it coherent, of inventing the type of coherence which we find here and is to be found in thousands of other rites, the coherence of the scapegoat mechanism whose repetition is attempted not because it is understood but because it is not understood.

Clearly other *bifurcations* are possible.[1] On the sacrificial slope, for instance, certain rites stress a single victim and a single sacrificial immolation, whereas others stress a collective participation in an undifferentiating mimesis.

In the latter case, the imitated system tends towards rituals of the *festive* or *anti-festive* type: rituals of uncontrolled eating, rituals of abstinence and privation. All the other aspects of the model may become – but do not have to become – the object of bifurcations; there are vocal rituals which tend to exclude actions, and there are rituals of action and participation that exclude pure spectatorship. Then there are the other rituals that tend more and more towards the latter and give rise to theatre and the plastic arts.[2]

Ritual imitation tends to concentrate on one aspect of the model, which it increasingly favours at the expense of all the others. It also transforms what it emphasizes. Ultimately, it engenders so many completely different forms that common sense revolts at the idea that they could all share the same origin.

There is nothing absurd about the common origin of both the king and the sacrificial orphan when considered in the light of the increasingly one-sided selective imitation of the dynamics experienced by Job. The idea of a common origin for all rituals does not defy common sense. Not only is the dynamic and transformational vision of rite that I have just outlined possible; it is the only probable one because it alone takes into account both the differences between rites and the common elements which remain to the end. No other theory has ever explained both these aspects of rituals.

In fact it is the only idea that can explain both the similarities and differences between one ritual and another, both the very pronounced and barely discernible differences that may be observed in neighbouring ritual systems.

The idea of a common origin seems fruitful to me as long as

it is conceived as a multiform and polyvalent event that appears highly complex and contradictory as a result of being misunderstood. Inevitably, it tends to become less complex as it is repeated deliberately, coldly, in the absence of spontaneous mimetic recurrences.

Nothing is more difficult to resolve in the cultural sciences than the role of analogy. In the nineteenth century, a great deal was made of the slightest analogies. Broad theories were derived from a limited number of misunderstood analogies. The results were obviously disappointing and the counter-reaction remains strong to this day. Since then analogies have been so mistrusted that people pretend, sometimes, not to see them. There is a refusal to draw the slightest conclusion from the most striking analogies for fear of experiencing the same old disappointment. Both attitudes are equally sterile.

We have just experienced a period in which the avoidance of analogies was considered scientific progress. Admittedly this attitude spares us the mistakes of the past, but unfortunately it gets us nowhere, as is evident from the current void. Without a mastery of analogies, no ethnological theorization is conceivable. And analogies can be neither overlooked nor avoided. We now cherish the illusion that progress in ethnology consists in no longer asking the essential questions and considering them irrelevant, especially in the religious domain. How long will we find this intellectually rewarding?

The real question is whether the common origin is a 'general idea' draped over the most diverse institutions like a garment that is too big and adapts itself to all shapes because it fits none, or whether it truly describes a genetic mechanism. With this as a starting point, can we determine geneses that are convincing and explain the details of institutions, taking into account what is different in analogous forms, as well as what is identical in different forms?

Taking analogies to be identities is a delusion, but rendering the analogous void by treating it as just another difference is an even more radical delusion. It is simply another way of avoiding the central problem of all research in the domain of culture. Until now, this reduction of what is analogous to what is different has gone unnoticed because it has been dictated by a linguistic approach which has promised to reformulate the problematic entirely. In fact, this approach merely evacuates the great questions of the past. Admittedly some of the earlier questions were not the right questions, but this is not true of others that are excluded along with them.

Analogy presents itself as a mixture of difference and identity, inextricable until today. Instead of seeking a direct solution to the problem, modern ethnology has wrongly thought that it could avoid it. In reality, it has only entrenched itself in two impasses: that of a delirious analogism, and that of an even more delirious 'differentialism'.

The thesis of violence and the sacred is not a return to a delirious analogism, which is all the delirious differentialism thinks it is. Rather, it is an attempt to get out of the twin impasse, to come to terms with analogy by virtue of a particular conception of *mimesis* and the scapegoat mechanism.

Many scholars fear that the thesis of a common origin must inevitably minimize or remove differences. Yet this does not really follow. Admittedly, until now, no single origin has produced convincing results, but *Violence and the Sacred* is not an origin in the sense that is rightly criticized today. If that book is mistaken, it is so in a new way. Even if it does not err by excessive analogism, differentialism will accuse it of this anyway. By distinguishing no difference among differences, differentialism ultimately dispels itself in insignificance and boredom.

To be aware of how the mimetic-scapegoat thesis takes 'differences' into account we must follow, step by step, the journey leading from the violent origin to the diversity of rituals, institutions and cultures. We must not be content to consider that journey impossible *a priori* for so-called anti-dogmatic reasons, since no dogmatism is as dogmatic, terrorist, and destructive of thought as blind anti-dogmaticism.

Scholars who wrongly think that classification is the ultimate goal of research cannot find anything of interest in my efforts, but the truel goal of research is to understand what we can explain, and to explain what is understood. The possibility of going beyond what can be classified, of tracing its genesis, seems to them impossible and contrary to clear and distinct ideas. Like former religious thought, the human and social sciences today remain Platonic in spirit. They transform the interconnected religious and social phenomena into independent essences.

Why is it impossible for these sciences to recognize the mechanism of collective violence even in a text where it is displayed as spectacularly as in the Dialogues of Job? Because their methods of analysis and ways of discrimination and differentiation remain subordinate to scapegoat mechanisms. They are constantly directed towards more and more subtle differences, away from the origin on which they depend.

Our languages are constructed to contrast the mimetic with the spontaneous. They assure the reciprocal exclusion of religious and non-religious behaviours, with only the latter perceived as being significant. They perpetuate the misappreciation of sole culprit mechanisms.

The Book of Job proves this limitation in the human and social sciences: the invisibility of the central phenomenon literally stares us in the face, but completely eludes secular methods of research as well as the theologies that remain sacrificial, the former being the continuation of the latter.

The scapegoat mechanism certainly differentiates: it produces the original differences; it differentiates Job as guilty, makes him the sole culprit among all his mimetic doubles, his fraternal enemies who call themselves friends; but it is not differentiated in the sense of ritual and post-ritual forms that could spring forth from it if all else were conducive. That is why the mechanism is not perceived by the kinds of ritual and post-ritual knowledge which still persist among us. We call them social sciences. To them, the mechanism seems like some sort of monster that resembles too many things at the same time to be anything definite in terms of the type of analysis which the mechanism itself sets in motion.

For many experts, to understand sacrifice means being able to detect the classifications of a particular system that interests them and to abide by them. They consider as *a priori* false any theory based on distinctions or comparisons that do not belong in the language of the system they are studying. They avoid analogies.

It does not seem right to say, as I have done, that the collective-victim process, the scapegoat in the common sense, provides the matrix for all sacrifices. For the thesis short-circuits distinctions that are never abolished by the liturgical systems. It is easy, therefore, to maintain that I have no respect for the facts. Fortunately, Job does the same thing. He too makes unseemly comparisons. His metaphors constantly compare things that theoreticians who respect institutional rules do not consider acceptable.

Of course, one can always turn a deaf ear or follow the example of the 'friends', giving their arguments a modern twist. The Book of Job undoubtedly belongs to 'literature', and the orphan chosen by lottery is only a metaphor. The king is only a metaphor. I agree, but is there no truth to be drawn from literature and its metaphors . . . ? Is the metaphor of the king so incongruous, or is it not rather perfectly justified and where it belongs?

Is it a pseudometaphor, a surrealistic metaphor that goes to great lengths to juxtapose objects that are really foreign to each other in order to obtain a gratuitous shock, or is it a metaphor that juxtaposes two realities that are in fact similar, but whose comparison astounds us because of our ignorance? We have always failed to recognize the similarity of the compared details but, if we are attentive to the metaphor, we may perhaps understand something unknown to us. There are things known to the metaphors of the Dialogues that are unknown to the best ethnologists.

The seeming neutrality of non-literary sources is less rich and, ultimately, less worthy of our trust than great literature. Job is in a better position than we are to judge sacrifice. His metaphors make sense only in the light of the connecting link described in *Violence and the Sacred* between collective persecution and ritual sacrifice.

We cannot base this link's existence or nonexistence on indications that may or may not be present in the systems of liturgical codification. These systems clearly never broadcast the fact that they are rooted in violence. To grant their explicit testimony the last word in the matter of sacrificial theory is like asking Job's community if their scapegoat is really a scapegoat, and if the acts of violence of which he complains are as unjustified as he claims.

Must Job be denied the status of an innocent victim on the pretext that he is the only one to claim the title and that neither the three friends nor anyone in the community agrees with him? All the traditional interpretations continue this tradition of denial. The most effective denials are never the most explicit. We are willing to recognize Job as the victim of God, of the devil, of bad luck, of fate, of the 'human condition', of clericalism and anything else, provided it is never a matter of his neighbours – that is, ourselves.

This refusal to recognize the victim as victim, this eternal claim that humanity is innocent, is the ultimate truth behind our misunderstanding the Dialogues. Secretly, we always agree with the false friends who feebly pretend to take pity on Job and treat him as guilty, not only to make him their scapegoat but also to deny that this could be happening. The two always go together.

Philippe Nemo[3] is right in thinking that the commentators share in the friends' effort to reduce Job to silence and in their insistence on only marginal texts.

True anthropological knowledge cannot be limited to a repetition of the classifications belonging to the systems studied. It must account for them by means of a theory that is genetic as well as structural. The scapegoat theory does not confuse spontaneous persecution with ritual sacrifices any more than Job himself, but it allows for the recognition of a relationship between spontaneous persecution and all sacrifices. This relationship is both metaphorical and real. It is metaphorical in that every ritual act is a substitution of victims; it is real in that the substitute victim is also sacrificed, and is more than ever a scapegoat.

Beneath the apparent incoherence of the discourses that follow but do not respond to each other a superior coherence is revealed, but only on one condition: the difference of perspective must be interpeted to Job's benefit; Job's discourse must be preferred over the others; the revelation of the scapegoat must be taken seriously. It must, in fact, be accepted as *true*.

We can interpret both the speeches of the friends and the whole of the Dialogues in the light of what Job says, but the reverse is not possible. The friends' speeches shed absolutely no light on what Job says. There are two truths, relatively speaking, in the sense of 'relativism' and 'perspectivism', but there is only one when it comes to knowledge, and that is the truth of the victim.

The current desire to 'respect differences' reaches the point of putting all 'truths' on the same level. It basically eliminates the very idea of truth, seeing it only as a source of conflict. But if we put the 'truth of the persecutors' on the same level as the 'truth of the victim', there will very quickly be no difference or truth for anyone. The friends are perfectly 'sincere', but their 'truth' is the lynching of innocent people. It is also a mystification. The 'truth' offered by Job is quite different: it is an unconditional, absolute truth.

It is not enough to recognize the object of the debate, the collective violence that is about to descend on Job and already affects him; we must also recognize the two perspectives on this violence and, more importantly, choose between them. Avoiding participation is a deception. Any pretence at *impassiveness*, whether stoic, philosophic, or scientific, perpetuates the *status quo*, prolongs the occulting of the scapegoat, and makes us effective accomplices of the persecutors. Job is the opposite of this impassiveness. Far from being a source of ignorance, his passionate identification with the victim is the authentic source of knowledge as well as everything else. The true science of man is not indifferent.

In our day certain aspects of this knowledge, the knowledge of the victim, are too vulgarized not to be sullied and perverted, not to become the paradoxical instrument of a more subtle persecution. The unique character of modern times is revealed in the fact that, in the competition for public opinion, the position of the victim is now the most desirable. It is no longer the ancient posture of a suppliant struggling to arouse pity, but a claim for legal and even extra-legal rights.

This unique situation is a product of biblical influence. But we need not, like Nietzsche, become obsessed by mimetic *resentment*, so that we look on it as the legitimate heir to the Bible and even as its earliest inspiration. Resentment is merely an illegitimate heir, certainly not the father of Judaeo-Christian Scripture.

Beyond the misunderstandings, calumnies and encroachments of which it is the object, beyond the historical reversals and even the disasters that result, and beyond all that disfigures it in our eyes, the truth of the victim that we at last possess is the greatest, most fortunate event in the history of religion and the whole of humanity.

V
THE VICTIM'S CONFESSION

16

A Totalitarian Trial

Envy and mimetic rivalries are reabsorbed into the phenomenon of the scapegoat mechanism and are transformed into a positive religion – provided, of course, that there is no residual aftermath; or rather, provided that the hostility to the scapegoat is completely unanimous.

If there is just one exception, if even one single voice is raised in disagreement with the unison against the victim, then there is no guarantee of a favourable outcome. The drug loses its effect; the group's unity cracks. If the hatred appears in the least bit lukewarm, doubt may spread, comprising the cathartic effects on the morale of the community.

Reinforcement of the community is identical with the strengthening of socio-religious transcendence. But such reinforcement demands a flawless scapegoat mechanism, completely unanimous agreement that the victim is guilty.

So long as the victim lives, he is a part of the community; he can therefore participate in the unanimity forming against himself. The need for unanimity is the community's primary concern. There is no reason for him to be an exception. In fact, his assent is the most important of all.

The three friends try to obtain Job's assent to the verdict that condemns him. That is the true purpose of their mission, since the efficacy of the scapegoat mechanism depends on it. This is no abstract discussion of the question of Evil.

The three friends seek to consolidate the 'system of representation' based on the selection of Job as scapegoat. Admittedly they set about it in the wrong way, but the only other way is not to intervene at all and to allow scapegoat systems of representation to form and disintegrate of their own accord.

The system consists of whitening the community by blackening the scapegoat; to consolidate it, the belief in this mythic blackness must be strengthened. The most effective means, obviously, is the victim's confession, in due and proper form. Job must publicly admit his infamy, proclaiming it loudly and convincingly.

Look at Oedipus at the end of his tragedy. He keeps repeating that he is a horrible impurity, disgusting to both gods and men: what in Greek is called *miasma*. He demands his own expulsion with an enthusiasm that will eventually earn him the community's respect. His docility immediately gains him attenuating circumstances, first with the Thebans who are content to exile him, and then again, in our day, with everyone. Ultimately, the only reason he is allowed to live is his exemplary behaviour as a victim, which is quite the opposite of Job's.

The victim is expected to explain to his fellow-citizens all the evil that should in future be attributed to him. This facilitates everyone's adherence to the orthodoxy that is being developed. The strength of this adherence, in primitive societies, makes it possible to tie the final knot and make the scapegoat the principle of social unity, a god who is both harmful and beneficial.

On Job's level, the knot has already come loose. For some time the scapegoating process has no longer produced this kind of divinity, but the sacrificial crisis only renders more necessary the victim's enthusiastic and spontaneous adherence to the mimetic frenzy that dishonours and destroys him.

Every time a 'wicked man' presents himself, the community brings out the same unchanging ritual machine, but Job's insubordination upsets the scenario: the producers, obviously, did not anticipate this form of resistance.

The intervention of the fourth inquisitor, Elihu, helps us to understand the truly unheard-of quality of the event: a victim who stands up to an entire community. The scandal is so great that an indignant reader, I suppose, tried to suppress it by inventing the character of Elihu. The inability of the first three 'friends' to reduce Job to silence has put this eager supporter of the God of vengeance into a terrible rage.

Essentially, Elihu is so in agreement with the first three lynchers that he cannot imagine any other reason for their failure than incompetence. His resentment against him, as well as against Job, is a symptom of the exacerbation of the sacrificial crisis. Like all superficial reformers, he uses his own youth as his chief argument, the proof of his superiority. When the operation of the 'ancient trail trodden by the wicked' fails, there are always men like Elihu who complete its disruption by trying to make it work again.

A comparison between the Dialogues and Sophocles' *Antigone* will help us understand what is at stake in the debate. Everything in that tragedy hinges on a scapegoat operation that is a little too visible to succeed in playing its role; the problem, as always in such cases, rests on the lack of unanimity in the community's adherence.

Only the necessity for unanimity can explain the importance of Antigone's rebellion in Creon's eyes. Neither the young woman's personality nor her relationship with Polynices gives weight to her disobedience, but rather the break in unanimity. By showing that Polynices is no different from Eteocles, his fraternal enemy; by demanding funerals for both of them, Antigone prevents the sacrificial resolution Creon wanted. She prevents the hollowing out of a mythical difference.

There is not the slightest difference between the two brothers who died as they lived, in the hostile symmetry of doubles. They are as alike as the two drops of water in the *Menechmes*. They are the same twins of violence. If the Thebans were to understand that their scapegoat, Polynices, had been chosen arbitrarily, if they were truly to recognize him as a *scapegoat*, the scapegoating would not 'take'; the victim would not appear to be responsible for the discord that destroys the community. The community would not be rid of its evil.

Thus is tragic discord perpetuated: this is, in fact, what happens in *Antigone*; the failure of the scapegoating process constitute the tragic action. In the absence of a victim who is unanimously considered to be guilty, a sufficiently disguised scapegoat, tragedy rebounds and new doubles confront each other: Antigone and Creon, the armies of Eteocles and Polynices.

What is at stake is the same as for Job, except in his case Antigone and Polynices are one and the same person. The scapegoat himself denounces the arbitrary expulsion. Job is the Antigone of his own cause. He is expected to acknowledge the justice of his own martyrdom, and he refuses.

The three 'friends' demonstrate the same wary obstinacy with Job as King Creon does with Antigone. Violence is within their capability, but they cannot use it openly. It is important to obtain the victim's free consent to his punishment.

The inquisitors begin to soften their tone and resort to strategy. They alternate threats of assassination with vague promises of reinstatement. It is to this, I think, that we owe – through the intermediary of the prologue, naturally – the particularly fallacious interpretation of the three friends as comforters. The relative moderation of the three owes nothing to pity. The friends never forget that their goal is to break Job's resistance, without any apparent constraint.

If Job's consent appeared to be obtained by force, it would lose all its value in the eyes of the community. This strategy foreshadows modern propaganda.

Since they are not successful in officiating at a sacrifice whose majesty is undisturbed, the group, first consisting of three, and then of four, friends begins to resemble more and more a circle of police around a suspect. They are not quite executioners, but any form of intimidation or psychological pressure is acceptable to them in order to obtain the 'spontaneous confession' so precious to dictatorial societies. The failure of the process of sacralization weakens the truly sacred connotations. Thus everything I have said about a religious regime can and should be applied to other regimes as well – if not, properly speaking, to a judiciary regime, then to police states and totalitarian governments.

There are remarkable analogies between that universe and

ours. Something in Job reminds us of a certain decline of modern justice. Everywhere ideology decomposes the legal system, legal parodies multiply and prompt behaviour patterns like those of the three inquisitors at Job's bedside.

In societies that have so far been spared this disturbing evolution it is difficult to explain the importance totalitarian regimes attach to the semblance of justice, just as it is difficult to explain the relentless efforts of the friends to make Job confess. Comparison of the two mysteries helps to explain them both.

In both cases, the proof and guarantees needed by judicial systems which respect human rights are lacking. This is what the persecutors are after, in the form of the sincere agreement of the accused in their own condemnation without proof, in their annihilation 'without trial', as Elihu proudly states. This agreement must replace the proof.

A perfect agreement between the perspective of executioners and that of the victims must be secured. The existence of a single truth is at stake, a truth that is properly transcendent and would be binding for all men without exception, even those crushed in the triumph of its procession. It must be shown that this truth is so constraining that it eventually wins over even those who, having failed to appreciate it, must suffer the consequences. They must recognize that they have sinned and that all their suffering is justified.

The need for a consenting victim characterizes modern totalitarianism as well as certain religious or para-religious forms of the primitive world. The victims of human sacrifice are always presented as very much in favour of their own immolation, completely convinced of its necessity. It is this persecutor's point of view that modern neo-primitivism fails to criticize.

Totalitarian ideologies destroy belief in an impartial and sovereign justice, foreign to the conflicts of the earthly city. Regimes that triumph on the ruins of a systematically flouted code of justice can no longer avail themselves of it in time of need. They have destroyed the law's effective transcendence in relation to the individuals that make up society.

When this transcendence no longer exists to secure the

sovereignty and continuity of judicial institutions; when there is no principle invulnerable to rival ambitions, to the vicissitudes of history, and to the corruption or mediocrity of its representatives, something immeasurable has been lost. Either there is no longer any common truth or, to impose one, one must live it to the end and, if necessary, die for it just as one is ready to kill for it. One must become it, be its *incarnation*.

In totalitarian systems, the rulers tend towards this status of incarnation. They write only infallible books and articulate only inspired words. They are treated as the living truth, the sacred king. We call it the 'cult of personality'.

But when there are several idols, the slightest discord between them affects and compromises a truth that truly exists only in its privileged incarnations. In the conflict of idols we see the division and fragmentation of the sacred; ultimately the whole of society runs the risk of breaking up and decomposing. The physical victory of one faction over its rivals is not sufficient to re-establish the unity of truth.

The conquered must freely recognize their fault. A confession of guilt is needed that is not seen to be extorted by violence. The accursed must give their blessing to the malediction that strikes them. They are not asked to forgive – especially not to forgive, for this would imply that the persecution was not necessarily infallible. What is required is their enthusiastic agreement with the decision to destroy them.

This is precisely what the three friends ask of Job. The losers must recognize that they were always in the wrong and were traitors. They thought they were innocent but must acknowledge that they were from the start guilty of parricide and incest. They deceived the people into acclaiming them when they did not really incarnate the truth.

Once institutional transcendence is destroyed, it can be only precariously and temporarily re-established, by means similar to those of primitive societies also lacking permanent transcendence for the opposite reasons: they have not yet created it. Modern totalitarian societies have finally destroyed that transcendence; primitive societies had not succeeded in producing it.

In both cases there is only one recourse: the scapegoat mechanism. Before totalitarianism, modern societies had not managed to eliminate scapegoats but they had both forced the worst of their violence outside themselves and reduced the violence left within their boundaries. This modest progress has been compromised in our time by the growing virulence of international conflicts and the powerful return of the scapegoating process in both terrorism and totalitarianism.

The three friends are no more interested in truth than are Soviet prosecutors. They are there to persuade Job to recognize in public that he is guilty. It does not matter of what he is guilty, provided that he confesses it in front of everyone. In the last analysis, the unfortunate man is asked to confess that he has been struck by an infallible god rather than by fallible men. He is asked to confirm the sacred union of the unanimous lynching.

17

Retribution

There are other characteristics shared by both totalitarian trials and the process by which Job is made a victim. One of the most striking of these is the obliteration of memory, the desire to eliminate not only the scapegoat but everything that might remind us of him – including his name, which must no longer be mentioned.

In the world of religion, this sort of conduct is justified by the pollution spread by the scapegoat. It is considered so insidious and formidable that the slightest emanation, even a faint recollection such as merely recalling his name, might cause contamination. The victim is so impure that his path must be covered with sulphur and disinfectants, and the last traces of his presence on earth must be destroyed:

> His memory fades from the land,
>   his name is forgotten in his homeland.
> Driven from light into darkness,
>   he is an exile from the earth,
> without issue or posterity among his own people,
>   none to live on where he has lived.
> His tragic end appals the West,
>   and fills the East with terror.
> A fate like his awaits every sinful house,
>   the home of every man who knows not God. (18:17–21)

There is nothing more ritualistic and traditional than this abolition of memory, the radical annihilation of the pseudo-guilty. In our era this demand for extreme destruction reappears in a laicized form. Certain religious proceedings remind us of prophylactic measures taken against epidemics and, even today, medicine is often involved in this type of business. A whole primitive apparatus makes its reappearance in modern totalitarianism.

The radical elimination of the 'guilty' reminds us of the manipulation of history in the totalitarian world. In the days of Stalinism, the disgraced leader became a nonperson and his name disappeared from the encyclopaedias and official annals.

There are no commemorative plaques along the 'ancient trail'. All that remains is the memory of the trail itself in the form of a vague threat hanging over all citizens which, in the case of Job, becomes more definite. Everyone who displays 'wickedness' in the eyes of those who manipulate public opinion is in danger of taking a little trip along this trail. In Job's case, the definition of 'wickedness' is his refusal to give in, his independence of judgement, his determination not to yield to the terrifying mimesis of the herd.

The cult of personality and parodies of legal process are not merely a question of unfortunate but excusable 'deviations'. Rather they suggest a relapse into social forms based directly on the scapegoating process. Because of ideological complicity many people are led to minimize what is happening, and that too is part of what is happening. They are persuaded that the 'deviations' will end once and for all on the day when the 'good' seize power and chase the 'evil' away for ever – in short, on the day when the 'good' alone will be in charge of the purifying expulsion.

This relapse into a type of social form that has un-questionably controlled most of human history is totally lacking in 'authenticity', and we do not know whether we should consider it less dangerous or, on the contrary, even more dangerous because of this. Whatever men do in future they cannot forget the scapegoat dimension of the Judaeo-Christian revelation. The reactivation of the scapegoat mechanism is always clumsy and suffers from its obvious falsehood.

The conscious element of manipulation is stronger in

totalitarian worlds that were formerly Christianized than in those that were never aware of the truth of the scapegoat. Our contemporary world revives primitive violence without rediscovering the absence of knowledge that endowed former societies with a relative innocence and prevented them from being unlivable.

When modern societies which have increasingly distanced themselves from primitive religion over the centuries without ever making a complete break yield to totalitarian temptations, they again come close not to primitive religion but to its disintegration. Possibly they surrender increasingly to these temptations for reasons that are inaccessible to narrowly political and even sociological patterns of thought.

It is no accident that the texts most capable of enlightening us on what is happening are the great texts that belong to the tragic and prophetic universe, the works most inspired by the sacrificial decadence of the ancient world. People are fond of saying that there is no need to 'make a tragedy of things', but perhaps we are caught up precisely in the tragic in its strongest sense.

This is why the Book of Job strikes such a contemporary chord. As our understanding of the victim's function in the primitive world grows, we shall be more able to penetrate the nature of human relationships in the totalitarian world. In both cases, the essential is the same unique absence that goes unnoticed because it is the absence of a thing that is not a thing and that many do not see. Its existence and importance are often discovered too late, at the moment when it ceases to be and as a consequence of its absence.

I am speaking of a social transcendence that is so strong and stable that it has no need of constant recourse to the scapegoats within a threatened group. Most Westerners are too protected by this transcendence to imagine the possibility of losing it and the undeserved privilege they still enjoy.

Any society in which the scapegoat resumes his immemorial role of founder and restorer of transcendence is totalitarian; but biblical and Christian knowledge has brought an awareness of the implications of the scapegoat that makes impossible the revival of the illusion of Job's friends, and of all those who believe they live in a flawless universe. The friends naively describe a universe governed by infallible justice, a universe that is undoubtedly atrociously cruel. Even without a lapse into neo-primitivism, we can admit that the unshakable conviction of those who inhabit such a world implies a kind of innocence and freshness lacking in the stifling totalitarian parodies of the modern world.

The demand for absolute perfection might well provide the common ground between the society of Job's 'friends' and current totalitarian societies. Faced with imperfections too obvious to be denied and with all that obviously fails to function correctly, the first reaction of totalitarian society is judicial rather than pragmatic. In order to find concrete solutions, the most fruitful state of mind is to think that perhaps no one is 'guilty'. To learn to cure the plague, one must first renounce the oracles of Laius and the hunt for a scapegoat. Totalitarian worlds renounce that renunciation. Unwittingly they reintegrate, in the name of 'progress', the state of mind so well defined by Eliphaz:

> Can you recall a guiltless man that perished,
>   or have you ever seen good men brought to nothing?
> I speak of what I know: those who plough iniquity
>   and sow the seeds of grief reap a harvest of the same kind.
> A breath from God will bring them to destruction,
>   a blast of his anger will wipe them out. (4: 7–9)

It is easy to understand why the three friends think as they do. They have always participated with the lynchers, as members of the community, in the episodes Eliphaz is describing. The Righteous are those who have never been lynched and who end up as well off as they began.

Generally speaking, those who are lynched are not around to talk about it: that is precisely what makes the speeches of Job an extraordinary exception and an abomination for an entire universe that can see in his complaints only an unforgivable subversion of the very idea of divine justice.

In the eyes of the friends, so long as there is no Job to trouble the enactment of the scapegoating process, everything is clearly best in the best of worlds. It is other men who are always pursued by divine vengeance; obviously, only the wicked are trampled by the crowd. Under these conditions, is it not natural to think that the world is extremely well made?

Those who are enveloped by the scapegoat mechanism, and completely convinced by it, live in a world that always conforms to the demands of Justice. If, momentarily, this world ceases to be just, sooner or later the scapegoating process will intervene to re-establish its perfection. The friends confirm this in the case of Job, just like the narrator of Psalm 73. Sometimes the celestial armies are a little slow to get going but, once in motion, they are quick to settle the accounts of the wicked. Ultimately, good and evil here below always receive what they deserve from God. Such is the power of the idea of retribution: an essential aspect of every system of mythological representation. A bit of reflection reveals that it is entirely based on the mechanism of a victim.

This is why belief in retribution dominates primitive religion. It is much more than a philosophy or even a theology. By primitive I mean every society that is structured on scapegoat mechanisms that are still intact. Transcendent justice is the same as the scapegoating process described by Job, so long as there is no Job to interfere by describing it. It is therefore as natural as it is supernatural, as transcendent as it is immanent. It is always there, for it is identical to mimetic unanimity, and eventually mimetic unanimity is always re-established in opposition to some victim or other.

On this point as on so many others, the revelations of the Book of Job are invaluable. The three friends could not believe as they do in the culpability of Job and all previous scapegoats without believing equally in an absolute Justice that always triumphs in this world. The two are one and the same. All those whom the whole community perceives to be guilty are in fact punished and all those who are punished, or seem to be punished – perhaps quite simply by a mishap – are immediately perceived to be guilty, and also become scapegoats. Justice inevitably triumphs.

The well-oiled scapegoat mechanism generates an absolutely 'perfect' world, since it automatically assures the elimination of everything that passes for imperfect and makes everything that is violently eliminated appear to be imperfect and unworthy of existence.

There is no room in this world for unpunished injustice or unsanctioned evil, any more than there is a place for the just person who is unlucky or the persecuted person who is innocent. This is what Eliphaz says. This circle has no break: the principle of this perfection will never discover what is fallacious about it. The mimesis is too strong. Job can go on yelling to the end of time without making his friends or anyone else understand.

The generative principle cannot be subverted. As soon as anything appears that might uproot it or make it seem illusory – like the voice of Job proclaiming that he is a scapegoat – the mechanism of elimination is set in motion, either in a primitive physical form, as is shown in Job, or in a derived, attenuated and intellectualized form of which the thousand ways of disregarding what Job is saying provide excellent examples. The fact that every 'system of representation' closes in on itself is ultimately a result of the scapegoat mechanism.

The tendency to attribute society's imperfections to scapegoats both within and without is certainly universal but, instead of discouraging and denouncing it, totalitarian societies foster and systematize it. They nourish with victims the myth of their own perfection, which they wish to promote.

18

Job's Lapses

Job often tends to magnify the number of his persecutors and exaggerate their strength. Remember that 'worthless brood' that lived on 'ravines' steep sides' or in 'clefts in the rock'. They are so exhausted by deprivation that they can barely stand. It is difficult to imagine what they have in common with the innumerable armies sent by the all-powerful to punish his enemies. We are not likely to confuse the two groups.

Without the slightest transition, the tone changes irresistible forces rush to the attack, and innumerable hordes sweep away Job's weak defences. Once more the epic of vengeance begins, but it is not the aggressors who have changed, it is Job who has shifted modes. A moment earlier he had been describing his enemies as 'enfeebled', capable only of spitting on him from nearby, then suddenly we find ourselves watching a charge of the Walkyries, as if one of the friends were speaking.

I will quote from the passage just preceding the end of the text mentioned above:

> And these are the ones that now sing ballads about me,
>   and make me the talk of the town!
> To them I am loathsome, they stand aloof from me,
>   do not scruple to spit in my face.
> Because he has unbent my bow and chastened me
>   they cast the bridle from their mouth.
> That brood of theirs rises to right of me,
>   stones are their weapons,
>   and they take threatening strides towards me.

They have cut me off from all escape,
    there is no one to check their attack.
They move in, as though through a wide breach,
    and I am crushed beneath the rubble.
Terrors turn to meet me,
    my confidence is blown away as if by the wind;
    my hope of safety passes like a cloud. (30: 9–15)

Without any apparent reason, the style of true revelation is replaced by epic exaggeration. The change occurs suddenly, in the middle of a tirade.

The heavenly armies are not imaginary. I pointed them out earlier. They are identical with the community in arms against the scapegoat. The linguistic weaknesses in Job confirm this. The adversaries are always the same. There is no radical shift in content. The nature of these linguistic slips removes any lingering doubt concerning the real identity of these famous armies. The real-life executioners and the supernatural warriors are one and the same.

In the texts already quoted, there was always a clear contrast between the speeches of the friends and those of Job. Here they are confused. I concentrated first on the most revealing texts, in which the realism of the scapegoat prevails. There are others that are quite different.

My global interpretation is based on the irreducible character of the contrast between the speech of the friends and Job's realism. There is on the one hand the persecutor's vision of society that gives birth to mythology and ritual, and on the other Job's vision that subverts the former by revealing that he is an unjustly persecuted scapegoat.

But here we have Job somehow crossing over to the enemy, imitating the ferocity of the friends in all the texts that show him faithful to the God of scapegoats, the barbaric God of the tribe.

All this produces an impression of chaotic disorder. For the readers who are seduced by the prologue and do not recognize Job as the scapegoat – harried on every side, pursued by an accusation that is wrapped in the mantle of divinity – his verbal lapses clearly contribute enormously to the misreading of the book as a whole and the amazing interpretative paralysis through the ages. They strengthen the authority of the God of vengeance and make the text inextricably enigmatic. As soon as a victim adopts the language of his persecutors, it is more difficult to recognize him in his role as victim.

In some of his speeches, Job is so like his adversaries that the textual editors are confused. They attribute to one of the friends statements that seem unlikely to be spoken by the hero.

The editors are probably right. There must have been interpolations, all kinds of manipulations, but the disorder is too profound for a purely philological solution. A general problem of interpretation is encountered here. In some cases, it is clearly Job who is speaking; we cannot replace him with one of his friends and yet he speaks exactly like them. He sounds just like Eliphaz, Bildad or Zophar in one of their fits of vengeance.

Yet we must not be swayed by this, nor lose the thread of violence and the sacred. The mixture of voices and the confusion of differences – all at Job's expense and to the benefit of the communal or totalitarian vision – far from compromising the reading I have suggested, fit it easily.

Job, at times, seems unable to uphold his realistic and revelatory discourse. He is the only one presenting this argument: the temptation to give up and say the same as everyone else may become irresistible. From time to time, he gives in. From the perspective of the totalitarian trial suggested in the previous chapter, these sudden verbal shifts could appear to be lapses on the hero's part, partial victories for the persecutors.

There is nothing easier than getting a suspect to admit anything when one knows how to go about it. A group's unanimous pressure on a solitary individual is bound to have an effect.

As Job weakens, he tends to borrow his adversaries'

language and repeats after them all the stereotypes of semi-ritual curses intended for 'wicked men'. Nothing in the text indicates or justifies these aberrations, but they are not in the least surprising.

Confused speech in a person subjected to so much violence is almost inevitable. Mimetic contagion between the victim and his executioners is normal. The mirror effects between Job and the 'friends' result from that strange force that sometimes makes even the most resolute victims succumb to the fascinating power of their executioners.

Some of Job's phrases strongly suggest the psychological phenomenon I have mentioned:

> Though I think myself right, his mouth may
>   condemn me;
> though I count myself innocent, it may
>   declare me a hypocrite.
> But am I innocent after all? Not even I know
>   that . . . (9: 20–2)

His strongest convictions begin to waver and are almost destroyed as a result of his friends' harassment.

We are in the same domain as before, both ancient and modern: the domain that Dostoevsky and Franz Kafka explored so brilliantly. Even in a world where social unanimity is not officially recognized as divine, it usually has an easy triumph over any individual resistance. This is not always true in Job's case, and that is what makes him an exceptional victim.

Should we believe that Job's strengths and weaknesses are deliberately created effects, cleverly calculated by an author capable of subtly suggesting emotions he himself does not feel: Job's disarray, his uncertainty, the complex intersubjective and spiritual situation I have tried to describe? Possibly, but not probably.

It is more likely that the author himself, faced with his own friends Eliphaz, Bildad, Zophar, etc., finds himself in a situation that is symbolically similar to the one he presents. He objects, and gropes towards something other than a violent God, without being fully in control of his own enterprise. I agree with Philippe Nemo that this is the correct and most exciting hypothesis to adopt. Everything in the Dialogues supports it, although it cannot be really confirmed. We are not aware of the author's exact relationship to his character, how close or distant he is. All we have is this character, and it is this character that we must discuss. Nothing prevents us, in talking about him, from imagining the unknown author of the Dialogues.

So Job reaches the point where he doubts his own innocence:

> If I resolve to stifle my moans,
> change countenance, and wear a smiling
>   face,
> fear comes over me, at the thought of all I
>   suffer,
> for such, I know, is not your treatment of
>   the innocent.
> And if I am guilty,
> why should I put myself to useless trouble? (9: 27–9)

This trait is characteristic of victims subjected to torture: their perception contains certain distortions that are always more or less similar to those of their persecutors. In the latter's vision of themselves, as in that of the victim, they become more formidable than they are in reality. An analogous phenomenon occurs in the specifically religious domain. Instead of rejecting the idea imposed on him that it is God who is his enemy, Job accepts and even defends it in a spirit of desperate pride.

Believing that he is the object of personal hostility on the part of God is the most terrible experience for the victim, but curiously it also offers a sort of compensation that he cannot be deprived of by the executioners, since the victim is adopting their own idea. To contradict him would be to contradict themselves. In order to regain a superiority over his persecutors that they cannot take away, the victim goes one better.

A similar situation can sometimes be found among individuals accused of witchcraft. Instead of denying vigorously their pacts with the devil, they find a sombre glory in them. It is a luxury that is costly to the prisoners, since it provides the persecutors with everything they are seeking. It legitimizes the accusation and completes the unanimity of violence.

Here is a characteristic passage:

> Will you never stop tormenting me,
>   and shattering me with speeches?
> Ten times, no less, you have insulted me,
>   ill-treating me without a trace of shame.
> Suppose that I have gone astray,
>   suppose I am even yet in error:
> it is still true, though you think you have
>   the upper hand of me
>   and feel that you have proved my guilt,
> that God, you must know, is my oppressor,
>   and his is the net that closes around me.
> If I protest against such violence, there is
>   no reply;
>   if I appeal against it, judgement is never
> given. (19: 2–7)

At the same time as he once more reproaches his friends for doing everything possible to crush him and prove his guilt, Job minimizes the role of human persecution compared with its divine counterpart, yet the latter is only concretized in the former. Only the attitude of men is responsible for revealing to Job God's hostility towards him.

Note the image of the divine net that imprisons the victim, found frequently in the Psalms whenever the scapegoat speaks, and also in epic and tragedy. Before killing Agamemnon, Clytemnestra robs him of his strength by throwing over him a kind of net which completely envelops him. The net resembles the surrounding of a victim by an armed troop. Although it is carried out by Clytemnestra alone, with the assistance of Aegisthus, the king's murder conceals a collective dimension symbolized by the net, like the permanent presence of those collective killers, the Erinyes, surrounding the murderers.

This image belongs to a cluster of metaphors centred on the hunt, preferably in its collective forms, such as a big-game hunt reminiscent of the manhunt. Agamemnon's net is to Orestes what Job's is for all the images of traps, hunts and nets in the speeches about the celestial armies.

What we encounter here is in each instance the god of the manhunt – not the prophetic Yahweh, but the tragic Apollo or Dionysus. This divinity is nothing but the fever of persecution that possesses the human group and is transmitted mimetically from one to another. He is the God of the friends. From a religious perspective, Job can hardly be distinguished from those around him in most of the Dialogues:

> Yes, God has handed me over to the godless,
> > and cast me into the hands of the wicked.
> I lived at peace, until he shattered me,
> > taking me by the neck to dash me to pieces.
> He has made me a target for his archery,
> > shooting his arrows at me from every side.
> Pitiless, through the loins he pierces me,
> > and scatters my gall on the ground.
> Breach after breach he drives through me,
> > bearing down on me like a warrior. (16: 11–14)

Again we see in this passage the *all against one* of collective violence: it is a matter once more of an epic/ritual account of the hunt for the scapegoat. God is certainly a single figure and, when he becomes a warrior, remains so; but this single figure is the equivalent of a group, for these warriors who surround the victim with their weapons are necessarily numerous. In speaking of the divinity, Job relies on the grand style of the celestial armies.

He says that God delivers him to the unjust and casts him into the hands of the wicked. At the same time as the victim confirms that his friends are persecutors he also, without being asked, maintains that he is really the victim not of men, but of God. Like everyone, Job cannot imagine that the whole populace can hate him without divine goading.

An old religious instinct prevents him from doubting his persecutors' right to appeal to the social God. Even though they are the 'wicked' and Job doubts their authority as men, he does not question their being people mandated by God: God himself has delivered him to the wicked. He endeavours to challenge the sacred authority of the lynching and to separate the divine from the human persecutors, but for the most part he is not successful and his language remains within the system of violence and the sacred. Even in his mouth we find magnificent definitions of the divine as the transcendent expression of collective violence.

Given the formidable mass of material we have accumulated, I wonder how critics can continue unanimously in their unawareness. What appears to be most incomprehensible is, in fact, the key to everything. The unanimity in question here can only be mimetic and this always repeated unanimity has been maintained through successive readings, both religious and non-religious. I doubt if this current effort will do anything to change the pattern.

To return to my argument, Job the conformist remains true to what he has always believed. He himself acknowledges that his prodigious popularity in the past came directly from God. He cannot recognize proof of divine benevolence in his worldly triumphs without equally acknowledging, in his overthrow by the people, the proof that God himself has cursed him. He continues to think in the same terms as the community.

For Job, the unanimous voice of the community is identical with the voice of God: *vox populi, vox dei*. The Latin adage provides a strict definition of the scapegoat system. We should not be surprised to see Job weakening from time to time in the point of his greatest strength: his protest of innocence. What would be amazing would be a lack of weakness on his part.

On the religious plane, things go so far that it is not enough to speak of 'lapses' or 'weaknesses'. Most of the time, Job cannot avoid the thought that has always been his – the thought of all those around him.

Religion is defined by the mimetic adoption of the actions and language of everyone, first in relation to the scapegoat and then in relation to everything that evolves from the process of ritual; religion is culture itself. In one entire dimension of his being, Job remains deeply immersed in his cultural universe. Having been chosen by the people, he inevitably thought he was chosen by God; he believes he is accursed on the day when he is cursed by the people. Is this so difficult to understand? Are things that much different in our society?

In the religious domain, tradition is at its strongest, cultural stability is greatest and innovation the least likely. Even in his very worst moments, Job does not yield completely to the unanimous public opinion that sees him as guilty; even in his best moments, he never manages to free himself completely from the fierce theology that overwhelms him.

The reader who judges the case from the prologue would expect to see a Job in grief, but less anguished than he actually is. To understand that anguish, it is not enough to recognize that Job is truly persecuted by men; we must also understand that most of the time he thinks he is persecuted by God himself. He is sufficiently in agreement with the terrible prejudices of his community to be all the more terrified. He is imprisoned by the tremendous coherence of the religious system from which, during most of the Dialogues, he does not succeed in separating himself: 'Fear comes over me, at the thought of all I suffer, for such I know is not your treatment of the innocent' (9: 28).

In most of the Dialogues, the God of Job is not the Yahweh of the Bible. Philippe Nemo has said it very well. One would almost be tempted to refer the reader to Durkheim had he not made an evanescent phantom of his sociological God by depriving him of the essential, amputating all the primitive qualities – the madness, implacability, compulsion and irresistibility – conferred by the scapegoat mechanism.

Every community in ferment against a scapegoat has seen its experience as the perfect example of a divine epiphany. And the scapegoat himself, even the exceptional scapegoat that Job is, only partially escapes such an interpretation. This is a great disadvantage in the battle he is waging to establish his innocence. He admits it himself. Men's arguments weigh less heavily with him than the concept of a divine sanction behind the human accusations.

Even our parallel to the totalitarian process leaves something to be desired. It encourages us rather to minimize the power conformism exercises over Job. In societies with violent religions men are not united against the scapegoat by an ideology, no matter how tyrannical, but by a powerful experience of the sacred, consolidated by an immemorial tradition. This vision is as binding as scientific evidence is in our day.

Yet what has become of Job's audacity, which seemed so very great a moment before? It seems to have slipped through our fingers. Yet it subsists. Despite the lapses I have mentioned, Job never gives in on the question of his innocence. His lapse does not last, and to the very end he will refuse to admit to any guilt. His final speech bears the stamp of unshakable certainty.

The victory is partial: since Job is incapable of directly confronting the notion that God is destroying him, he resorts to the weapon of the weak: he protests.

If he cannot reject this God in his entirety, Job can repudiate various fragments and aspects of him; he can subvert and challenge sacred authority on specific points. Since he is put in the position of the accused, he in turn arraigns God and attacks, above all else, the divine justice.

Job is driven to revolt against this social God who is unacceptable to him, but remains the only God he can imagine. He accuses this God of delivering him 'to the godless', and throwing him 'into the hands of the wicked' without any reason, and without allowing him any opportunity of defending himself:

Yes, I am man, and he is not; and so no argument,
  no suit between the two of us is possible.
There is no arbiter between us,
  to lay his hand on both,
to stay his rod from me,
  or keep away his daunting terrors.
None the less, I shall speak, not fearing him:
  I do not see myself like that at all. (9: 32–5)

Since I have lost all taste for life,
  I will give free rein to my complaints;
  I shall let my embittered soul speak out.
I shall say to God, 'Do not condemn me,
  but tell me the reason for your assault.
Is it right for you to injure me,
  cheapening the work of your own hands
  and abetting the schemes of the wicked?' (10: 1–3)

In his most desperate moments, Job tries to seduce his friends
and enlist them in a sort of alliance against God. He tries to
tear them away from the divine cause which he claims they
defend with false arguments. Anyway, God does not need
them:

Will you plead God's defence with
prevarication,
  his case in terms that ring false?
Will you be partial in his favour,
  and act as his advocates? (13: 7–8)

Again we are shown the same effort to separate the two inseparable entities, God and the community united against him,
with the same lack of success. How could Job succeed in
detaching such conventional individuals, who behave like
sheep, from a cause that he always recognizes, either implicitly
or explicitly, as that of God?

Job is incapable of doubting the existence of this mimetic

God who demands victims, so instead he frantically attacks his so-called justice. He claims that the God of the scapegoat is unjust with him, the individual called Job, but he does not limit himself to his own case; it is clear to him that if he speaks only about himself he will convince no one. He argues universally:

> When a country falls into a tyrant's hand,
>   it is he who blindfolds the judges.
> Or if not he, who else? (9: 24)

Instead of seeing justice everywhere in the world, as Eliphaz does in the long passage on retribution quoted above, Job sees injustice everywhere. He reverses the schema of the social God. This reversal is easily explained within the framework of the tremendous attack, an attack that is sometimes both hasty and confused, mounted by Job against the entire system of victimization:

> Why do the wicked still live on,
>   their power increasing with their age?
> They see their posterity insured,
>   and their offspring grow before their eyes.
> The peace of their houses has nothing to fear,
>   the rod that God wields is not for them.
> No mishap with their bulls at breeding time,
>   nor miscarriage with their cows at calving.
> They let their infants frisk like lambs,
>   their children dance like deer.
> They sing to the tambourine and the lyre,
>   and rejoice to the sound of the flute.
> They end their lives in happiness
>   and go down in peace to Sheol. (21: 7–13)

Job similarly ridicules the theme of the good death reserved only for the just. This theme fits the idea of retribution like a glove and makes it obvious that the roots of this idea lie in the scapegoating process.

Dying well means dying as late as possible, 'ending their life in happiness', but most of all dying surrounded by everyone's admiration, enjoying up to the very end the respect of fellow-citizens without which life would not last long, and in any case would not be worth living. The theme has been emphasized in too many other biblical and non-biblical texts not to be rooted in a vague fear of coming to a bad end. Coming to a bad end, of course, does not always imply being lynched but dying abandoned and despised by everyone – a death that is not foreign to abandonment and scorn.

At the time when the people worshipped him, Job thought that adoration would accompany him to his death and that he would never lose his prestige. He says it all the time:

> My praises echoed in every ear,
>   and never an eye but smiled on me; [. . .]
> So I thought to myself, 'I shall die in
> honour, [. . .]
> My reputation will never fade,
>   and the bow in my hands will gain new
>   strength.' (29: 11; 19–20)

For a leader of the people a good death is not to die as a scapegoat, but to be venerated even in death. For the powerful of this world, the men on whom is focused the envious mimesis of a thousand rivals, the theme of untarnished prestige and the participation of many people in the funeral ceremonies is too important not to indicate their fear of ending up as 'wicked men'.

Job thought he was destined for a good death; he believed in retribution as long as he believed in the loyalty of his admirers, but he believes in it no longer. It is not surprising that Job, rejected by his people, should fight the idea of any equivalence between popular favour and the real merits of an individual. According to the new Job, the Wicked benefits from the advantages automatically reserved for the Righteous through a complete and unbroken system of victimization:

But who is there then to accuse him to his
face for his deeds,
 and pay him back for what he has done,
When he is on his way to his burial,
 when men are watching at his grave.
The clods of the valley are laid gently on
him,
 and a whole procession walks behind him. (21: 31–3)

In this upside-down world, the Wicked finish well and the Righteous badly. This sort of argument finds no echo among the 'friends', of course. They possess irrefutable proof that Job is mistaken: the victim is Job.

Since the three friends are always in agreement with the crowd, for them the crowd's verdict decides who is just and unjust. They, therefore, have never seen nor will ever see a Wicked man coming to a good end or a Righteous man coming to a bad end. Everything is always perfect for a humanity mystified by the periodic eruptions of its own unanimous violence.

Evil reveals its intractable character in this world only when the scapegoat mechanism is challenged and destroyed. My interpretation is therefore compatible with Philippe Nemo's. My only wish would be for him to pay greater attention to man's responsibility for the sufferings of the rejected idol.

19

'My Defender Lives'

We have seen nothing as yet on the religious plane that reflects the audacious revolt of the scapegoat. In all the passages quoted, Job's religion remains imprisoned by the mimesis of scapegoating. God continues to be for Job what he is for everyone around him: the mythical entity to which all episodes of violent unaminity are attributed.

If there were nothing else, we would be forced to conclude that Job's audacity is purely 'existential', lacking in any truly religious efficacy. But there are two exceptions to the rule outlined. Two great texts shatter the conformity we have just observed.

God suddenly appears to be listening to Job's outcry. A witness for the defence stands at his side, a defender of the Righteous who have been unjustly treated. Perhaps Job's protests have reached God. The accusers, the Satans, are no longer the only ones to be heard. God lends an ear to the victim:

> Henceforth I have a witness in heaven,
>   my defender is there in the height.
> My own lament is my advocate with God,
>   while my tears flow before him.
> Let this plead for me as I stand before God,
>   as a man will plead for his fellows. (16: 19–21)

These lines no longer reflect mimetic submission to the God of violence, nor its contrary, a revolt that perpetuates the reign of that God. For once despair gives way to hope, which would never have occurred had not the very concept of God changed.

To observers as influenced by biblical values as we are, what is happening here seems so banal that it is difficult to recognize its originality. The reason I have laid so much emphasis on the haunting presence throughout the Dialogues of the God of persecution, even in the speeches of Job, is to bring out this originality and make tangible the religious about-face taking place in the few words I have just quoted.

This about-face on the part of a universally rejected victim does not surprise us. Deprived of all human support, the victim turns to God; he embraces the concept of a God of victims. He does not permit his persecutors to monopolize the idea of God. We live in a world where nothing is easier or more natural than this appropriation of God by the victim.

In relation to public opinion, in our world the most advantageous position is almost always that of the victim. Everyone tries to occupy it, frequently without any real justification. But this possibility, used and abused by us all, we owe to the Bible. The texts we are reading have contributed heavily to its conception.

These texts are themselves the reflection of a quite different universe in which the violent form of the sacred maintains its hold over the greater part of the Dialogues, including some of Job's statements. The solemnity of the passages in which that hold slackens suggests a keen awareness in the author that he is articulating things never heard before.

The unanimous community considers that it can judge without proof or trial: its own bloody turmoil is seen as a divine inspiration. As we have observed, no one is excluded from that communion – not even the victim, provided he justifies the violence and is not a spoilsport. But a victim who defends himself to the end, a victim who prevents that communion and thwarts the divinity, seems inconceivable. How could he also claim to have the divinity on his side?

Job does not go so far as to repudiate the God of the persecutors. But he installs at his side not the accuser, Satan – whom this God *is* already by definition – but his opposite, a representative of the accused, an advocate for the defence.

This God does not then become the exclusive God of the victims – that is unthinkable – but he is no longer exclusively the God of the accusers and persecutors. The text of the ecumenical translation (Revised Standard Version) seems to make this duality clear by suggesting a real opposition inside of the divinity:

> Even now, behold, my witness is in heaven,
>   and he that vouches for me is on high.
> My friends scorn me;
>   my eye pours out tears to God,
> that he would maintain the right of a man with
> God,
>   like that of a man with his neighbour. (16: 19–21)

This first text leaves the God of persecutors and the God of victims in each other's presence. But a second text extends the movement that seems to be interrupted in midstream in the first. The two aspects of the double divinity cannot be balanced or stabilized. They are incomparable and incompatible. Three chapters later, the movement is resumed and Job takes another step in the direction of the unthinkable: a God of victims:

> This I know: that my Avenger lives,
>   and he, the Last, will take his stand on earth.
> After my awaking, he will set me close to him,
>   and from my flesh I shall look on God.
> He whom I shall see will take my part:
>   these eyes will gaze on him and find him not
>   aloof. (19: 25–7)

This time, God is openly on the side of Job: he intervenes on behalf of the victim but only after Job's death, and perhaps after the death of all men, to do justice to the one who has been unjustly condemned. It would seem that at the end of time, a living relationship will be established between God and the

Righteous man who has been wronged. Job will be at home with God, justified and consoled for his misfortune.

These two passages constitute the high point of the Dialogues. The revelation of the victim who proclaims his innocence must provide their substructure, since the mimetic certitudes of the scapegoat mechanism must be shaken in order to conceive of a God of victims. But this remains implicit. There is nothing elsewhere in the Dialogues or in the rest of the book that reaches the height of these two texts.

The God who finally breaks silence and answers Job 'from the heart of the tempest' does not make the slightest allusion to the questions posed in these two passages, or to Job's protestations of innocence. He does not seem to understand that Job is the victim of his community; or perhaps he is pretending. Job, for his part, is an individual who is engaged in a metaphysical protest without valid reason. With this speech, he cuts short the whole problematic of the scapegoat. This God poses the problem in the deceptive way that has prevailed ever since: he pushes aside anything that has to do with Job's relations with his community – the best way of neutralizing the subversive force of Job's speech. The words remain, but their meaning becomes almost inaccessible. This is much more effective than reducing Job to silence by a too-obvious physical violence.

To escape the formidable hornet's nest of human relationships, this God takes refuge in nature. He lectures Job at length on what used to be called natural history. A little astronomy, a little meteorology, and a lot of zoology. This God loves animals. He holds forth inexhaustibly on the ibis, the cock, the lion, the wild donkey, the wild ox, the ostrich, the horse, the falcon, and finally on Behemoth and Leviathan. The latter are the chief stars of this menagerie. They bear a strong resemblance to a crocodile and a hippopotamus, lightly garnished with mythological inspiration.

The poetry of this bestiary should not conceal from us that it constitutes a display of irresistible power. This God demonstrates his strength so as not to have to use it. He is no longer the God of the friends, who openly oppresses against scapegoats. He no longer brandishes the celestial armies against the rebel.

He resorts to cunning and wins his case: Job is finally docile and silent, full of terrified admiration for the ostrich and Leviathan. Each animal takes its turn, and the scapegoat admits he is free of his sorrows. It is difficult to take this farce seriously. All the interpreters are critical of it, yet it plays a role in smothering the Dialogues.

After the failure of the three friends, and then of Elihu, the God of the animals is only a supplementary reinforcement for yet another rehash of the scapegoat scenario. Persecution is no longer exercised against Job, but on the preceding revelations that this God's conjuring trick has made seem insignificant and academic. Job's speeches are transformed into that pitfall of the question of Evil which has remained the focus of universal exegesis for thousands of years.

The operation that failed on the level of real violence succeeds totally on the textual level. On the religious plane, this God is merely a less openly ferocious variant of the God that preceded him. Since he does not reveal the scapegoat mechanism, it follows that he is rooted in it.

This sort of showman who passes for God has nothing in common with the Defender to whom Job appeals. The Job who gives obsequious thanks to this charlatan has nothing in common with the Job of the Dialogues. It is difficult to recognize this passage as a legitimate sequence to the Dialogues and acknowledge complete satisfaction with Job's satisfaction.

Like the prologue and the conclusion, the only purpose to the speeches of this God is to eliminate the essential and make the Dialogues unreadable, to transform the Book of Job into a ludicrous anecdote recited mechanically by everyone.

The God of the final speeches remains the God of the persecutors but less visibly, in a more hypocritical manner than the general at the head of the celestial armies. He conceals his game cleverly, all the more so because he himself has no understanding of it.

In place of the celestial armies, only Behemoth and Leviathan remain. Only this God's taste for monstrous force still suggests indirectly what was too naively demonstrated by the torment of a single victim surrounded by divine warriors.

This God's speeches are as foreign to the true grandeur of Job as the prologue and conclusion. What neither the three friends, nor the fourth, were able to obtain from Job is achieved by this version of the God of persecution recycled into an ecological and providential God. Job agrees to acknowledge everything and anything. This certainly cannot be attributed to the author of the Dialogues.

All the additions to the Dialogues do violence to the original text; they are victorious acts of persecution in that they have succeeded, until now, in neutralizing the revelation of the scapegoat. Everything that is not Job in the Book of Job, with the powerful support of the exegeses forming a vengeful circle around the Dialogues, endeavours to conceal the essential message: to falsify it or, better still, to bury it again, suppressing it entirely.

All the additions to the Book of Job and the additions to the additions that constitute the proliferous interpretation (almost exclusively directed towards what predicts and resembles it – the prologue, Elihu, the speeches of God and the epilogue) offer the textual equivalent of the 'celestial' armies, bent on a single victim. Here the scapegoat is speaking through the voice of Job; that is what must be silenced: the same effort is constantly required to bring about the effective functioning of the mechanism that Job is preventing.

These additions deserve all the evil that can be said about them – but some words of praise also. They isolate the Dialogues, wrapping the same protective coating around them as posterity always unfolds around the prodigious scripture, and the result is not purely negative.

Job's virulence has never had the powerful effect on cultures influenced by the Bible that it might have done, but beneath the protective coating that shelters and protects it from us just as much as from the real Job, this virulence has remained intact.

By concealing Job's subversive power, the mystifying additions have made the text accessible to ordinary devotion and, at the same time, prevented it from being rejected in horror, or so completely censored, changed and mutilated that its meaning would be lost for ever. By protecting the texts from too rough a contact with a hostile world and serving as shock-absorbers, these additions and commentaries that falsify have made possible the preservation of the texts that no one reads, since they are meaningless within the context given them. If the extent of their subversiveness had been more visible, they might never have survived for us.

The value of these additions and commentaries is that they do not aim at total censorship of the Dialogues; the authors want to adapt the text for purposes of assimilation. They are making Job acceptable to the various orthodoxies. They sense in him a genius that exceeds them and the manipulations and even sacrificial mutilations they accomplish are of limited significance. They do not want to eliminate the name of Job, but rather to moderate his formidable strength. They are like those insects that paralyse their victim but take care not to kill it in order to preserve a substance that later, much later, will provide exquisite nourishment for their progeny.

The epilogue drowns the scapegoat in the puerile acts of revenge of a Hollywood success story. It is worth little more than the prologue, and yet contains one remarkable sentence. After speaking severely to the three friends God adds that, in consideration of Job's merits, he would not refuse to relent towards them or inflict his disfavour on them 'for not speaking truthfully about me as my servant Job has done' (42: 8).

Only Job has spoken the truth about God, by apparently insulting him and denouncing his injustice and cruelty – whereas the friends, who always spoke in his favour, had spoken badly of him. We should read in this sentence a profound judgement on the Dialogues in their entirety. This epilogue is, of course, correct, but it is so timid and mystifying on the whole that its boldness in this sentence is astonishing.

The only God that Job attacks is the God of the lynchers.

The conclusion does not make this essential distinction; it does its best to make it invisible but this approval given to Job must be based on some insight into the truth which cannot reach the conceptual level.

Although this conclusion contributes to the disfiguration of a text whose genius is disturbing, it does not totally repudiate that genius, but renders it homage. It fails to see what distinguishes Job from his friends; it does not perceive the abyss between the God of executioners and the God of victims. It cannot reach our conclusion that only the former is being attacked by Job. But it nevertheless understands that Job's revolts stem directly from biblical inspiration.

Unlike Claudel, who reproached Job for his blasphemies, this conclusion prefers Job's erring to the conformity of the friends. It does not want to be totally deprived of that spiritual effervescence. For all its lack of exegetical power and mystical intuition, this conclusion has flair. We should recognize in it what is called the *sense of orthodoxy*.

20

'A Bloody Ransom to Still the City's Frenzy'

The God of the persecutors has a logic of his own, and the God of victims must have his also. If conceived with rigour, what would he say to men, how would he behave towards them? Let us try to develop the logic of this God.

Certainly he would want to put an end to the religion of violence and the persecution of innocent people. How would he set about doing this?

Without thinking about it, our immediate reaction is that God in his omnipotence would use his divine powers to prevent violence and injustice. If violence and injustice nevertheless continued to exist, he would put an end to them and restore things to their previous state. This God of victims, in other words, would acknowledge the just claims of Job. Instead of mobilizing his armies against the scapegoat, he would mobilize them against the persecutors.

Mythology provides interventions that appear to correspond to such a schema. Look, for example, at the intervention of Zeus on behalf of Dionysus, a similar affair to Job's but on the scale of the Titans. Together the Titans massacre and devour the child, but they receive their just punishment: Zeus strikes them down and restores the innocent to life. Should we recognize the God of victims in Zeus? Of course not. Like all the Greek gods, Zeus is a god of vengeance and violence.

Just for once the innocent is avenged and the wicked punished, whereas in the Book of Job the reverse is true. But what can the innocent victim gain from this vengeance? And in Job's case, who can say what is right? If Job's cause were to triumph through violence, how would it differ from the justice of Eliphaz or Elihu? What persecutors do not consider themselves the guiltless avengers of innocent victims? A little mimesis is enough for men's vengeance to be completely confused with that of God. God is always the one who

> . . . smashes great men's power without inquiry
>   and sets up others in their places.
> He knows well enough what they are about, . . . (Job 34:
> 24–5)

The God who avenges Job against those who are jealous of him and restores him to the throne would be no different from the God who destroys 'wicked men', or from Zeus who strikes down the Titans. The justice claimed on Job's behalf is not much different from the justice celebrated by Eliphaz and Elihu when they compare Job with the 'wicked men'. Whenever there is group mimesis, invariably the 'good' win out and the 'evil' are punished.

But where, then, can we look for the true God of victims? Where can we look for the God who will put an end to these horrors? We should certainly mention the Athena of the *Eumenides* among the possible candidates. I was rightly criticized for her absence in *Violence and the Sacred*.

In Aeschylus' *Eumenides* the law of lynching lies at the heart of the drama, as it does in the Dialogues. To rid ourselves of the law will be a difficult undertaking since, among the Greeks as elsewhere, collective murder produces religious values.

The Erinyes certainly do not symbolize only 'remorse' or obsessional phenomena, corresponding to nothing external and therefore susceptible to psychoanalytical interpretation. They signify – as is unambiguously stated in the tragedy and confirmed by Aeschylus in the subsequent text – a vengeance that is collective and social rather than individual, even when it is the work of a single individual. Orestes, for example, acts in the name of the city that is totally in revolt against Aegisthus and Clytemnestra, who are merely the power of a moment, the idols of the day. Again we encounter the 'ancient trail trodden by the wicked', the process described in Job which psychologists and more paradoxically sociologists – and even Hellenists, the specialists in Aeschylus – have failed to see.

The Erinyes represent collective murder very explicitly and they must abjure it solemnly if it is to disappear. This abjuration transforms them permanently into the gentle and fruitful Eumenides. Athena assumes responsibility for bringing this about. Without the confession on the part of the religious forces directly associated with the original violence, any modification of the system would be only illusory. The transformation would be merely in appearance only.

This is the promise of the Erinyes:

> This I pray: May faction, insatiate of ill,
> never raise her loud voice in this city.
> May not the dust that drinks the black blood of
> citizens
> in its passion for vengeance,
> demand a bloody ransom to still the city's frenzy.
> May joy be exchanged for joy
> in a common love
> and may we hate with a single soul:
> for this is man's great remedy. (trans. from Jean Grosjean, *Eumenides*, Pléiade, p. 409)

This text is a major document on generative violence. What is translated here as 'faction' marks the event to which Job's friends constantly allude and which they brandish over his head, like a menace, without ever identifying it except by euphemisms such as 'the King of Terrors' or 'the ancient trail trodden by the wicked'. It is the peak of the mimetic crisis, the climax of the crowd's agitation that results in the scapegoat mechanism, the moment when there occur all the acts of disorder and violence preparatory to the paroxysm of the scapegoat. The latter is the object of a precise definition: 'the bloody ransom' that must be paid to put an end to the 'city's frenzy'.

All this requires the utmost attention, but particularly the last two lines, which are truly amazing. Evidently the poet is thinking of the danger of disintegration a city might risk when deprived of the savage means of collective violence. Would this city, by the same token, be deprived of the great *remedy* provided by unanimous hatred? Does it not risk decay?

Aeschylus is clearly aware of the effect of collective violence on the city of men, both in its primordial forms that range from the cannibalism of Atreus and Thyestes to Orestes' matricide – all of which are to be found in the three tragedies of the *Oresteia* – and in its derived forms, to which in future it must be limited.

In order to reassure his public, or himself, Aeschylus maintains that hatred will neither disappear nor lose its power of creating unanimity when it is no longer crystallized in the primitive form symbolized by the Erinyes.

The principle of this world, in other words, can be perpetuated under other, less horrible, forms than 'faction' and its 'bloody ransom'. There is, therefore, no serious obstacle to the elimination of it all.

The horrible forms produce more and more scandal in a *polis* that is well policed and, in any case, their fruitfulness is exhausted. All attempts to end vengeance have failed. Murders follow murders from one tragedy to another without ever bringing the slightest peace. It is this crisis that forces violence to change, to continue under less savage forms, forms that are more adapted to the historic circumstances, in a world renewed by more effective legal strictures.

Aeschylus recognizes implicitly the generative role of mythological murder, since it remains obscurely in the 'civilized' forms that should be substituted for the type of murder so formidably portrayed in the *Oresteia*.

But for this continuity, the Erinyes would not be defining this new universe in which joy and love play a greater role but from which their counterpart, hatred, will not be eliminated.

This new world will know how to make hatred a force for unity, the *great remedy*, identical with, but other than, the terrible force for division it constitutes *so long as it is not unanimous*. Aeschylus understands the crucial importance of unanimity.

What is merely insinuated by the definition of the mechanism, two lines earlier, is made completely explicit by the last two lines: the bloodshed for bloodshed puts an end to the city's frenzy. It is redeeming in that it renders hatred unanimous; by providing men with the means of hating with a single soul, it brings them the *great remedy* for communal life. This is Aristotle's *catharsis* in its original form. Now we must turn to derived forms of which tragedy, evidently, is one. This is the reason for which the tragic poet can speak authoritatively on this subject.

There cannot be a more authoritative expression of the thesis of generative violence and its derived forms than that of Aeschylus. The whole operation of cultural origin is as clear here as in the Dialogues of Job. These two great works, the Greek and the biblical, say the same thing about aspects of this operation such as the social and religious function of unanimous hatred. Remember Job's tirade about the 'public Tophet'. The convergence of these two testimonies gives us reason to reflect.

We cannot reproach Aeschylus for entertaining the illusions of our rationalists about his contemporaries. The Athenians need not worry. They can renounce, without further thought, the barbarous relics of the past. They will be sure to find other objects of unanimous hatred. Perhaps Aeschylus is thinking about a foreign war.

After every successful 'bloody ransom' and as a result of unanimity, the Erinyes, by becoming the Eumenides, as had already happened in the past, continue to symbolize the spirit of collective hatred and vengeance. The difference is that there will be more joy and love. There will always be collective hatred:

> May joy be exchanged for joy
> in a common love
> and may we hate with a single soul:
> For this is man's great remedy.

Nowhere in the Bible will we find the idea that the city of man should accommodate itself to generative violence, making room for it under the pretext that 'much wrong in the world thereby is healed'. In a movement that might well be termed pre-totalitarian, as in certain dialogues of Plato, Aeschylus becomes the *shepherd* of that violence. This is Heidegger's profound and violent meaning when he speaks of the *shepherd of being*. The latter, for some reason, has always made me think of the wolf in disguise of the fable. Beneath the pure white coat of the sacrificial lamb, one black paw is showing.

The single soul of hatred: this implies the hatred experienced by all citizens simultaneously for the same individual or group of individuals. Aeschylus does not express this clearly.

Everything said by Aeschylus presupposes the selection of a scapegoat, even an arbitrary scapegoat, but neither his work nor that of the Greeks in general ever mentions it directly. A scapegoat is essential to the system's functioning, but it is a question not of the scapegoat himself, but of a system based on a scapegoat.

Only the Bible speaks of the victim as a victim. There is no question of anything else. The various schools of interpretation are no more interested in this difference than most of the religious exegetes. Job's complaints, and the endless complaints of victims, make the Bible intolerable for many people, perhaps for everyone.

Paradoxically, only Nietzsche pays attention to the voice of these victims. But he does so only in order to overwhelm them even more, and accuse them of 'resentment'.

Interiorized vengeance, the 'reversed' vengeance of sinful Christians, is certainl, a terrible evil, but one would have to be the spoilt child of the Bible and of Hellenism in Aeschylus' sense, and have truly forgotten the taste of black blood in the dust, to look for a new *great remedy* for resentment in a return to real vengeance, as Nietzsche does, both consciously and unconsciously. Nietzsche inverts Aeschylus in a crazy fashion. Nietzsche is truly mad, but no one notices it in a world where every effort is made to catch up with him in respect of this madness.

The comparison of Job and Aeschylus leads to the same conclusions as that of Job and Sophocles: the same insight on the topic of generative violence but, among the Greeks, the community rather than the individual victim always wins.

The two great insights in the Book of Job into the God of victims have no equivalent among the Greeks. They are isolated, as I have pointed out, even in our biblical text. Everything in their context conspires to limit their reach. The God who is supposed to answer Job at the end of the book represents a kind of strategic retreat along the lines of the Eumenides, a fresh effort to re-establish a sacrificial system discredited by Job, which cannot be re-established in the shape of mob murder as Eliphaz describes it. The God of victims would not respond to the persecution by making the scapegoat into an extremely rich stockbreeder.

The conclusion of the Book of Job encourages in us a desire for revenge that considers itself morally superior because it champions a rehabilitated scapegoat, but it is no more than a softened and inverted version of the celestial armies. If we want to rid ourselves of the system of action and representation based on the scapegoat, commemorating victims and indulging in loud lamentations over them, which we are so good at doing – all the while calling ourselves 'Nietzscheans' – is not enough. On the contrary, it is by the infinite play of substitutions, modifications, subtle transfigurations and wily inversions that the scapegoat system has succeeded in enduring until now and still dominates our thought today, even as it convinces us that it is nonexistent.

The god of Behemoth and of Leviathan pretends to be the God of that innocent victim, Job; but he remains the God of persecutors, the God of the modern Eliphaz, somewhat the God of everyone, just as the Eumenides remain the goddesses of vengeance even after having been recycled into civilization. This progress should be neither overestimated, as it was after Aeschylus, nor underestimated, as it is by contemporary intellectuals in the wake of Nietzsche.

We have not been able to find anywhere the God of victims

that Job longed for. The true greatness of Job, like that of the Psalms, is the existence, side by side with the still-present hope for vengeance, of a hope for the God of victims. Job has started something that remains incomplete.

Perhaps the expression 'God of victims' is only a trap. What is the significance of the God of victims, the God of the weak and oppressed? At the end of our study of Job, we recognize the extraordinary difficulties implied by such a notion.

21

The God of Victims

The God of the Gospels is clearly a candidate for the role of the God of victims. The Father sends his Son into the world to defend the victims, the poor, and the disinherited. In the Gospel according to John, Jesus calls both himself and the Holy Ghost a Paraclete. The word signifies advocate for the defence in a law-court. It should be compared with the word that the Jerusalem Bible translates as 'avenger' in the last text of Job I quoted, the Hebrew word *goel*, a legal term with a similar significance.

Jesus is systematically presented as the Avenger of victims. He proclaims that we cannot come to the aid of the least among them without coming to his aid, too. We cannot refuse to give aid without also refusing it to him.

Is the God of the Gospels the God of victims? The title is not necessarily warranted simply because it is claimed. It is appropriate to consider whether the logic of this God that has so far escaped us is truly developed in the Gospels.

As we have seen, a God of victims cannot impose his will on men without ceasing to exist. He would have to resort to a violence more violent than that of the wicked. He would again become the God of persecutors, supposing he had ever ceased to be. Every persecutor believes he knows the true God of victims: for them he is their persecuting divinity.

If there is a God of victims, we cannot count on him to bring about a world that everyone would agree to call just. Otherwise, the agreement of men is based on poor reasons. Even their most pacific agreement is mixed with mimesis. However just, their injustice is mixed with vengeance, which again is another word for mimesis.

When Job proves that justice does not hold sway in the world, when he says that the sort of retribution Eliphaz implies does not exist for most men, he thinks he is attacking the very concept of God. But in the Gospels, Jesus very explicitly claims as his own all Job's criticisms of retribution. And clearly the conclusion is not atheism:

> It was just about this time that some people arrived and told him about the Galileans whose blood Pilate had mingled that of their sacrifices. At this he said to them, 'Do you suppose these Galileans who suffered like that were greater sinners than any other Galileans? They were not, I tell you. No; but unless you repent you will all perish as they did. Or those eighteen on whom the tower at Siloam fell and killed them? Do you suppose that they were more guilty than all the other people living in Jerusalem? They were not, I tell you. No; but unless you repent you will all perish as they did.' (Luke 13: 1–5)

According to the Jerusalem Bible, 'the meaning of both is clear; sin is not the immediate cause of this or that calamity' (Note 13a to Luke 13: 1–5). The atheists who take up Job's arguments against retribution are closer to the Gospels than Christians who are tempted to use the arguments of Eliphaz in favour of that same retribution. There is no necessary connection between the evils that strike men and any specific judgement of God.

Persecutions are real persecutions and accidents are real accidents. As for hereditary weaknesses, that is all they are – hereditary weaknesses. Because they attract the attention of persecutors, they are always seen as the sign of divine condemnation. Jesus rejects such a religion. To the disciples who ask him whether the blind man was born blind because either his parents or he had sinned, Jesus answers: 'Neither he nor his parents sinned . . . he was born blind so that the works of God might be displayed in him' (John 9: 2–3).

All the parables have much the same meaning. God always

plays the role of the absent master, the owner who has gone on a long journey. He leaves the field free for his servants, who prove themselves either faithful or unfaithful, efficient or timid. He does not allow the wheat to be separated from the tares, even to encourage the growth of good grain, whereas Aeschylus does the reverse. God makes his sun shine and his rain fall on the just as well as on the unjust. He does not arbitrate the quarrels of brothers. He knows what human justice is.

Does this mean that the God of victims is some kind of lazy god who refuses to intervene in the world, the *deus otiosus*, traces of whom are believed by certain ethnologists to be found in the pantheons of many primitive religions, the god to whom no sacrifice is made because he can do nothing for men?

Absolutely not. This God spares nothing in order to rescue victims. But if he cannot force men, what can he do? First he tries to persuade them. He shows them that they are dedicating themselves to *scandal* by their desires that are crisscrossed and thwarted by imitation.

Jesus enjoins men to imitate him and seek the glory that comes from God, instead of that which comes from men. He shows them that mimetic rivalries can lead only to murders and death. He reveals the role of the scapegoat mechanism in their own cultural system. He does not even conceal from them that they are dependent on all the collective murders committed 'since the beginning of the world', the generative murders of that same world. He demands that they recognize the sons of Satan, devoted to the same lie as their father, the accuser, 'murderer since the beginning'.

Jesus scarcely convinces anyone. His revelation receives just enough acceptance to invite suppression by whose who hear it. By revealing the truth, Jesus threatens the domination of Satan, the accuser, who in turn exerts on him the greater force of the unanimous mimesis of the accusation, the scapegoat mechanism. He becomes, inevitably, the victim of that same satanic force that, as accuser and persecutor, controls the world and has already killed all the prophets from Abel to the last victim mentioned in the Bible.

And that is what happens. All hate *with one soul*. Like Job, Jesus is condemned without being guilty and, this time, it is he who becomes the *'bloodshed for bloodshed . . . given our state to prey upon'*. Thus yet again there is reproduced, in the Passion, 'the ancient trail' that we have been discussing from the beginning.

If the God of victims intervenes on their behalf in the human world, then he cannot 'succeed'. All that can happen to him is what happens to Jesus and has already happened to Job and all the prophets. Jesus must find himself in Job's place, and not by chance. He is as innocent as Job and even more so, but by revealing how the world functions, he threatens its foundations more seriously than Job. That he finds himself in the position of a single victim results from a rigorous logic.

For an understanding of that logic, we must consider the implications of violent unanimity when it occurs. In that fundamental moment for human culture, there are only persecutors and a victim confronting them. There is no third position, no way out. Where would the God of victims be, if he were to find himself among men at that point in time? Obviously he would not be on the side of the persecutors, so he would have to be the victim. Rather than inflict violence, the Paraclete would prefer to suffer.

Christ is the God of victims primarily because he shares their lot until the end. It takes little thought to realize that nothing else is possible. If the logic of this God shares nothing in common with that of the God of persecution and its mystifying mimesis, the only possible means of intervention in the world is that illustrated by the Gospels.

According to the logic of the world, which is also that of the God of persecution and his cohorts, the failure is total. It would be better not to intervene at all than to choose this method of intervention. This God is worse than *otiosus*. He is the most miserable, ridiculous, least powerful of all the gods. It is not surprising that his 'impact' on the world decreases the less he is confused with the God of Eliphaz.

This God cannot act with a strong hand in a way that men

would consider divine. When men worship him they are almost always, unwittingly, honouring the God of persecutors. This God does not reign over the world. Neither he nor his real name is sanctified. His will is not obeyed.

Do I exaggerate this God's impotence? I am only repeating, verbatim, the words of Jesus to his Father:

> Hallowed be thy name.
> Thy kingdom come,
> Thy will be done on earth as it is in heaven.

This prayer would make no sense if the divine will – while remaining divine in the sense of the God of victims, while remaining itself – could break the obstacle created by men's will.

These words are prayers. God does not reign, but he will reign. He reigns already for those who have accepted him. Through the intermediary of those who imitate him and imitate the Father, the Kingdom is already among us. It is a seed that comes from Jesus and that the world cannot expel, even if it does all it can.

Another proof that God does not claim to rule over the world is that he reveals its king to us, and it is not himself but his adversary who is always eagerly in pursuit – Satan, the accuser and the persecutor. A little thought reveals that the defender of victims, the Paraclete, must have as adversary the prince of this world, but does not oppose him with violence.

The teaching of Jesus and the Passion in the Gospels constitute the strict development of a paradoxical logic. Jesus wants nothing to do with all that makes someone divine in the eyes of men: the power to seduce or constrain, the ability to make oneself indispensable.

He would seem to want the very opposite. In reality, it is not that he desires failure but that he will not avoid it if that is the only way he may remain true to the Logos of the God of victims. He is not secretly motivated by a taste for failure, but rather by the logic of the God of victims that unerringly leads him to death.

This logic permeates the Gospels through and through. The way it works is presented as a manifestation of the divine that is still hidden and radically different from the sacred of the persecutors. We are, then, confronted with yet another paradoxical aspect of the Logos of victims.

In a world of violence, divinity purified of every act of violence must be revealed by means of the event that already provides the sacrificial religion with its generative mechanism. The epiphany of the God of victims follows the same 'ancient trail' and goes through the exact same phases as all the epiphanies of the sacred of persecutors. As a result, from the perspective of violence, there is absolutely no distinction between the God of victims and the God of persecutors. Our pseudoscience of religions is based entirely on the conviction that there is no essential difference between the different religions.

This confusion has affected historical Christianity and, to a certain degree, determined it. Those who are opposed to Christianity today endeavour to perpetuate it by clinging desperately to the most sacrificial theology in order not to lose that which nourishes it and to be able always to say: Christianity is only one among many religions of violence, and possibly the worst of them.

The Logos of the God of victims is almost invisible in the eyes of the world. When men reflect on the way in which Jesus conducts his enterprise, they see little other than his failure, and this they see ever more clearly so that, inevitably, it is perceived as definitive and final.

Instead of denying that failure, Christian theology affirms it in order to convert it into a startling victory. Death becomes resurrection. The Logos that has been expelled 'makes it possible to become children of God' for all those who did not expel it, all who 'receive' him or – what amounts to the same – any victim rejected by men. The expulsion of the Logos is the beginning of the end of the 'reign of Satan'. Defeat in the world is really victory over the world.

The wisdom of the world sees in this reversal a deception that is easily demystified. Thus one says this is a compensatory figment of the imagination, an imaginary revenge on an uncompromising reality. Many modern Christians are more or less openly in agreement with this interpretation.

If Jesus' defeat were turned into a victory only in the afterworld, the question would be totally one of religious belief or disbelief. From our perspective, there would be nothing to add.

But according to the Gospels, the very world is threatened and the kingdom of Satan is about to disintegrate. If these words are in agreement with the Logos of the God of victims, then they must hold some significance within the context of our analyses.

It can be shown – or rather, we have just shown – that in fact these words have a meaning in the domain we are currently studying, the comparative analysis of religious texts. They are quite different from the imaginary revenge postulated by those who remain blind to the Logos of vicitims. The demystification they think they achieve is merely another scapegoat mystification.

Here and now, on the plane of ethnological and religious texts, the victorious reversal of the Passion provides us with something tangible that can be understood rationally. To understand this, one need only return to the exegetical advance in progress and extract from it the essential result.

We have discovered, at the heart of every religion, the same single central event that generates its mythical significance and its ritual acts: the action of a crowd as it turns on someone it adored yesterday, and may adore again tomorrow, and transforms him into a scapegoat in order to secure by his death a period of peace for the community.

This central event is decisive and yet so little known that there are no words to describe it. The human and social sciences have never discovered it. In order to describe it, we have borrowed the periphrases of the texts we were reading: 'the ancient trail trodden by the wicked . . . the bloodshed for bloodshed given our state to prey on . . .'

This event is also present in the Gospels, but on this occasion it does not just appear in transit: it is not only clearly described, but named. It is called the Passion. Jesus is the perfect victim, because he has always spoken and behaved in accordance with the Logos of the God of victims. He provides the only perfect image of the event which is at the root of all our myths and religions.

The passages of the Dialogues I have quoted form an amazing sequence that is very similar to what is called the 'public life' of Jesus, the 'public life' to which the Crucifixion, of course, belonged.

Job and Jesus differ on many points, but they are alike in that both tell the truth about what is happening to them. The resemblance lies not so much in the individuals as in the relationship of these individuals to the people around them. For reasons that are different but similar in result, it is the same for Job face to face with his people as it is for Jesus face to face with the crowds in Jerusalem and the various authorities who finally crucify him.

Like Job, Jesus enjoys a period of great popularity. The crowd wants to make him a kind of king, until the day when, through the mimesis of persecution, it turns against its idol with the same unanimity as Job's community did against him. The hour of violent unanimity has struck, the hour of absolute solitude for the victim. Friends, relatives, neighbours, all those whom Jesus has most helped, those he has cured, those he has saved, the disciples most dear to him – all of them leave him alone and, at least passively, join in society's outburst.

In the first texts I quoted, Job's neighbours, his servants, his slaves and even his wife criticize him, abandon him and ill-treat him. This is much the same as the agony of Jesus. It is the same effort on the part of the authorities, represented in the Dialogues by the friends, to make Job confess his guilt; and the same effort to consolidate the hostile opposition to the suspect.

In order to perceive the structural resemblances of the two relationships, we must see what they have in common and ignore the anecdotal and local differences. (My reference is to events, not to people.)

If the Christian text is allowed to intervene in the interpretation of the Dialogues, we immediately achieve decisive results. The futility of the boils and the lost cattle is apparent. The incredible originality of the Dialogues becomes more visible. The enigma of this text comes to light. And the Gospels provide what is needed to resolve that enigma, the knowledge of the Passion that is responsible for the essential articulation of the text, and reveals the true nature of the drama of Job's life.

Everything that Job's readers, with the help of the prologue and the epilogue, have managed not to see for two thousand years or more we will be forced to see through the accounts of the Passion, unless we yet again barricade ourselves against its message.

But this time, the meaning will penetrate. It is easy to fail to understand the experience encountered in reading only the Book of Job. But once we recognize the similarities between the experience of Jesus and those of the scapegoat Job, they cannot be forgotten.

The accounts of the Passion gather into one tight bundle all the threads of a structure scattered throughout Job. In the Gospels there are no cattle to distract us, no ostrich or hippopotamus to play hide-and-seek with the real problem.

If I have managed to recognize in Job a crowd that turns on its former idol and gathers in unanimity against a scapegoat – a sinister trial intended to stifle Job's protests – and if I attach importance to these aspects, if I emphasize them by drawing out their social and religious drama, it is because I have been guided from the beginning by the accounts of the Passion.

By this I do not mean that during these analyses, the Passion was explicitly present in my mind. That is not necessary. Whether we like it or not, the Passion is a part of our cultural horizon: it provides, as scholars would say, the 'structural model' through which the Dialogues can become ever more legible.

When we examine the Book of Job in the light of the Passion, we are immediately able to isolate the essential text, the Dialogues. The excrescences are no longer apparent that cling like warts to the face of Job and prevent us from perceiving the beauty, from discarding what is parasitical in the message about the scapegoat – all that conceals the guilt of all men, including our own, in seeking out scapegoats: the satanic principle on which not only this community, but all human communities are based.

There is an anthropological dimension to the text of the Gospels. I have never claimed that it constitutes the entirety of Christian revelation, but without it Christianity could scarcely be truly itself, and would be incoherent in areas where it need not be. Without this dimension, an essential aspect of the very humanity of Christ, his incarnation, would be missing; we would not perceive fully in Christ the victim of the men we all represent, and there would be the risk of relapsing into the religion of persecution.

For the Dialogues to be interpreted as they should, as I have already mentioned, we must choose the side of the victim against the persecutors, identify with him, and accept what he says as truth . . . As it has come down to us, the Book of Job does not insist enough on our hearing the complaint of Job: many things divert us from the crucial texts, deforming and neutralizing them with our secret complicity.

We need, therefore, another text, something else, or rather someone else to come to our aid: the text of the Passion, Christ, is the one to help us understand Job, because Christ completes what Job only half achieves, and that is para-doxically what in the context of the world is his own disaster, the Passion that will soon be inscribed in the text of the Gospels.

For the true significance of the Dialogues to become apparent we must follow the recommendation of the Gospels: pay attention to the victim, come to his aid, take note of what he says. Following the example of the Gospel text, Job's complaints must become the anchor for every interpretation and, very quickly, we will understand why Job speaks as he does, we will recognize his role as scapegoat, the double phenomenon of the crowd, the myth of the celestial armies, and the true nature of the social and religious mechanism that prepares to devour another victim. We can see how everything is linked and organized with extraordinary precision.

The only true reading is that in which Job's outcry becomes the indestructible rock of interpretation; but only through the Gospels can it be developed, only the Spirit of Christ permits the defence of the victim: he is therefore truly the Paraclete.

Most interpreters have always suspected that to do justice to the Book of Job, one must take the part of the unfortunate. Everyone therefore tries to defend Job, identify with him and praise him.

It would not be an exaggeration to identify this as the aim of the additions to the text, but they all fall short of that aim because of their lack of understanding of the community's role in Job's misfortune. Subsequent interpreters fall equally short, and will continue to do so as long as they do not turn to the one on whom even Job calls in the supreme moment of the Dialogues: the defender who is found at God's side, whom Christianity says is God himself, the Paraclete, the all-powerful advocate of all wrongfully condemned victims.

In saying this, it becomes clear that we are not dreaming, we are not falling into 'compensatory illusions'. The symbols we are using are actually in the text since they resolve the problems, rehabilitate the victims, free the prisoners and, above all, reveal that the God of this world is truly the accuser, Satan, the very first murderer. By coming to the help of Job and reinforcing the revelation of this unusual victim who is Christ, we are striking a death blow to a world system that can be traced in a straight line back to the most primitive forms of violence against scapegoats, the persecution of Job and the murder of 'Abel, the righteous'.

For centuries, now, the Passion has turned itself about as a triumph at the level of cultural understanding. It provides the interpretative grid by means of which we prevent texts of persecution from crystallizing into sacrificial mythology. In our own time all modernist culture, that bastion of anti-Christianity, begins to disintegrate on contact with the Gospel text. We owe all the real progress we have made in interpreting cultural phenomena to that one Revelation whose effect continues to deepen among us.

Far from being too ridiculous to be worthy of attention, the Christian idea that out of Christ's defeat comes victory has already been realized among us in the collapse of the culture of Marx, Freud and Nietzsche and in the heightened crisis of all the values that the post-Christian era believed were successful in their opposition to Christianity. 'The stone rejected by the builders has become the cornerstone.'

The relevance of the Christian text to the interpretation of Job has always been recognized, vaguely, by the doctrine that makes of the work a 'prophetic' book in the Christian sense, a book that heralds and prefigures Christ. The depth of this doctrine is apparent only in its earliest applications, the Gospels and the epistles of Paul. As we move forward in time and as these applications are multiplied in the Middle Ages, they become increasingly superficial.

The 'allegorical' readings are wrong in that they are satisfied with similarities between simple words, common names and even proper names, characters isolated from their context and thought to be prophetic of Christ because they are morally exemplary.

The more intellectually and materially comfortable Christianity became, the less it retained the memory of mimetic relationships between men and the processes that result. Hence the tendency of the early Christian exegetes to fabricate an imaginary Job who passes for a prefiguration of Christ for his moral goodness and his virtues, especially for his patience, even though Job in reality was the personification of impatience.

It is easy to ridicule the Christian concept of the prophetic. Yet, like all authentically Christian ideas, the *figure Christi* reveals a great truth, one that has been gradually discredited so that in our day it is completely rejected by Christians themselves, who alone are responsible for its relative sterility. They did not know how to take hold of the idea concretely and make it truly useful. On this point, as on so many others, the inability to maintain the Logos of the God of victims in all its purity paralyses the revelation. It contaminates with violence the nonviolence of the Logos and makes the latter a dead letter.

The truth of prophecy in the Christian sense appears from the moment mimetic processes are emphasized rather than characters treated as Christ figures.

Job foretells Christ in his participation in the struggle against the God of persecutors. He foretells Christ when he reveals the scapegoat phenomenon that envelopes him, when he attacks the system of retribution, and above all when he briefly eludes the logic of violence and the sacred in the two last texts quoted.

Job goes a long way along the path that leads from one logic to the other, from one divinity to the other. But he cannot really swing from one system into the other. Thus the solution that perceives in him a 'prefiguration' of Christ seems to me the most profound – providing, of course, the concept is supported by analyses that emphasize human relationships, as instructed by the Gospels.

The 'prophetic' becomes significant at the heart of an approach that is in no way retrogressive to 'traditional values', in the face of what would be the audacity of the modern subversive and *critique du soupçon*. For a new approach to the Christian text, that criticism must be radicalized: which is precisely the effect of the mimetic-scapegoat thesis. It cannot be said to make use of established values. There is nothing about it that is 'pious' in the traditional sense of the word.

Nothing is both more disturbing and more exciting than the irresistible resurgence of the Christian text, at a time and place when it is least anticipated.

In the New Testament, particularly Luke, knowledge of

Christ is frequently achieved in two phases. There is a first contact that results from a movement of curiosity and a purely superficial sympathy.

This is followed by disenchantment and disaffection. The disciple who is not completely converted feels he has been mistaken and distances himself. This movement of retreat will not be stopped, it is truly without return; yet it will put the person who despairs in contact with the truth, but a truth so profound that it is transfigured.

The eunuch of Queen Candace came to Jerusalem to have the Gospels explained to him. He returns discouraged, for he does not yet know who could be the Servant of Yahweh in the Book of Isaiah, that unjustly condemned scapegoat who saves the community. But Philip happens to come along and explains to him that Christ is the person in question. After being baptized, the eunuch 'went on his way rejoicing' (Acts 8: 26–40).

There is the same movement in the story of Emmaus. Two disciples are leaving Jerusalem after the Passion and are talking on the way about the collapse of their hope. Here again is the same attitude of sceptical and suspicious discouragement with regard to a revelation that has clearly failed. The discouragement even brings about its own reversal: at the destructive moment of suspicious criticism, suddenly Christ is walking with the disciples and explaining to them the Scriptures. But 'their eyes were prevented from recognizing him.'

We may one day understand that the entire history of Western thought conforms to the model of these two stories and to a third similar one, also found in Luke: that of the Prodigal Son.

Of these three texts, by far the most precious for those of us who spend so much time writing commentaries on them, interpreting them and comparing them, is the one about the road to Emmaus. It seems orientated towards the 'work of the text'; it does not even forget to include the rewards of this work, which the interpreter receives when the light finally dawns, coldly and even, in one sense, implacably rational and at the same time just the contrary, unnacceptable in the world's eyes, mad, truly demented, since it speaks of Christ, since Christ speaks through it, since it emphatically validates the most apparently absurd hopes, hopes that are considered culpable in our day. Does it not suggest that all our real desires are gratified simultaneously?

Then they said to each other, 'Did not our hearts burn within us as he talked to us on the road and explained the scriptures to us?' (Luke 24: 32)

Notes

1: Job the Victim of his People

1. Raymund Schwager, *Brauchen wir einen Sündenbock?*, Munich, 1978.

4: The Celestial Armies

1. See *The Scapegoat*, The Athlone Press, 1986, ch. 6, p. 92.

5: Realism and Transfiguration

1. René Girard, *Violence and the Sacred*, The Johns Hopkins University Press, 1977. *Des choses cachées depuis la fondation du monde*, Grasset, 1978. *The Scapegoat*, The Athlone Press, 1986.
2. See note 1.

6: Oedipus and Job

1. Meyer Fortes, *Oedipe et Job dans les religions ouest-africaines*, ed. J.-P. Delarge, 1974.
2. Trans. David Grene, University of Chicago Press, 1954, lines 463–82.
3. Sandor Goodhart, 'Oedipus and Laius, Many Murderers', *Diacritics* 8 (1978), pp. 55–71.

7: 'Jezebel Trampled to Death under the Horses' Hooves'

1. Jean Racine, 'Athaliah', Act I, Scene 1, lines 120–3. *Racine's Mid-Career Tragedies*, trans. L. Lockert, Princeton University Press, 1955.
2. Jean Racine, *Britannicus*, Act V, Scene 6, lines 1748–54, trans. John Cairncross, Penguin Books, 1967.
3. Jean Racine, 'Phaedra', Act V, Scene 6, lines 1568–77. *Jean Racine's four Greek plays*, trans. R. C. Knight, Cambridge University Press, 1982.
4. Jean Racine, 'Bajazet'. *Racine's Mid-Career Tragedies*, op. cit.
5. 'Athaliah', Act II, Scene 5, lines 503–6. *Racine's Mid-Career Tragedies*, op. cit.

8:'A Whole Country Possessed by Saint Vitus's Dance'

1. Saint-John Perse.

9: Psalm 73

1. Paul Dumouchel and Jean-Pierre Dupuy, *l'Enfer des choses*, Seuil, 1979; Jean-Pierre Dupuy, *Ordres et Désordres*, Seuil, 1982; Colloque de Cerisy, *l'Auto-organization*, ed. Dumouchel and Dupuy, Seuil, 1983; *Cahiers du CREA*, no. 2 (1983), 1 rue Descartes, Paris.

10: The Mountain Torrent

1. Eric Gans, *Pour une esthétique paradoxale*, Gallimard, 1976.
2. 'Mimésis et Morphogénèse', in *Ordres et Désordres, op. cit.*, pp. 125–85.
3. 'Le Signe et l'Envie', in *l'Enfer des choses, op. cit.*, p. 66.
4. Paul Dumouchel, 'L'Ambivalence de la rareté', in *l'Enfer des choses, op. cit.*, pp. 137–254; Georges-Hubert de Radkowski, *Les Jeux du désir*, P.U.F., 1980.

11: The Public Tophet

1. Except the text of Aeschylus at the end of the *Eumenides*. It will be discussed in Chapter 20.
2. Old Testament, Pléiade edition.

12: The Orphan Chosen by Lots

1. *Job et l'excès du mal*, Grasset, 1978.

14: Job and the Sacred King

1. A. Caquot, 'Les Traits royaux dans le personnage de Job', Maqqel Shadeqh. *Hommage à Wilhelm Vischer*, pp. 32–45.

15: The Evolution of Ritual

1. Jean-Pierre Dupuy, 'Le Signe et l'Envie', in *l'Enfer des choses, op. cit.*, p. 62.
2. All this makes possible and even demands detailed analyses that would take into account the formal differences.
3. *Job et l'excès du mal, op. cit.*, p. 28.

Index

171